Happiness

Daniel Nettle is Reader in Psychology at the University of Newcastle. His publications include *Vanishing Voices* (with Suzanne Romaine), *Linguistic Diversity*, and *Strong Imagination: Madness, Creativity, and Human Nature.* He runs the psychological research website www.psychresearch.org.uk

D0061952

Happiness

THE SCIENCE BEHIND YOUR SMILE

Daniel Nettle

OXFORD

UNIVERSITY PRESS

OXFORD
UNIVERSITY PRESS

Great Clarendon Street, Oxford OX2 6DP

Oxford University Press is a department of the University of Oxford.
It furthers the University's objective of excellence in research, scholarship,
and education by publishing worldwide in

Oxford New York

Auckland Cape Town Dar es Salaam Hong Kong Karachi
Kuala Lumpur Madrid Melbourne Mexico City Nairobi
New Delhi Shanghai Taipei Toronto

With offices in

Argentina Austria Brazil Chile Czech Republic France Greece
Guatemala Hungary Italy Japan Poland Portugal Singapore
South Korea Switzerland Thailand Turkey Ukraine Vietnam

Oxford is a registered trade mark of Oxford University Press
in the UK and in certain other countries

Published in the United States
by Oxford University Press Inc., New York

British Library Cataloguing in Publication Data
Data available

Library of Congress Cataloging in Publication Data
Data available

Typeset by RefineCatch Limited, Bungay, Suffolk
Printed in Great Britain by the
MPG Books Group, Bodmin and King's Lynn

ISBN 978–0–19–280559–1

5 7 9 10 8 6 4

Contents

List of figures

Happiness is an ideal not of reason but of imagination
IMMANUEL KANT, *GRUNDLEGUNG ZUR*
METAPHYSIK DER SITTEN

Life is a progress from want to want, not from enjoyment
to enjoyment

BOSWELL'S *LIFE OF JOHNSON*

Introduction

'We hold these truths to be self-evident,' wrote Thomas Jefferson in the American Declaration of Independence in 1776, 'that all men are created equal, that they are endowed by their Creator with certain unalienable Rights, that among these are Life, Liberty and the pursuit of Happiness'. Of these three, it is the third that seems most able to imbue our lives with purpose. Without its guiding light, there would be no way of knowing what to do with life and liberty, or so it would seem. Jefferson's rights one and two wake the horse up and open the stable door, but only number three—the pursuit of happiness—is going to make it go anywhere.

The idea that happiness is central to the point of the human experience goes back to the ancients. The Greek philosopher Aristippus argued in the fourth century BC that the goal of life is to maximize the totality of one's pleasures. If this is true, which is more debatable than it might seem, then happiness becomes the overarching explanatory concept in all of psychology, and surely the most urgent of personal questions for any human being to solve. More than this, happiness also moves to the centre of political and economic decisions. If maximizing happiness is the point of individual lives, then the point of systems of government and economy should be to maximize collective or aggregate happiness. This position is a pure form of the doctrine of Utilitarianism, which was made famous by moral philosopher Jeremy Bentham (1748–1832), but foreshadowed in the thought of Francis Hutcheson who claimed, 'That action is best, which procures the greatest happiness for the greatest numbers'.

This form of utilitarianism has an enduring appeal. The government of the Himalayan kingdom of Bhutan recently announced that the goal of public policy there would be to increase not the Gross National Product, but the Gross National Happiness. The Bhutanese are obviously on to something. Happy people live longer than unhappy people and are less vulnerable to disease. And there are enduring differences in happiness between nations, between the rich and the poor, and between the married and the single. However enlightened it may seem, though, the Bhutanese strategy immediately raises questions. Can people's happiness actually be changed by public action? Come to think of it, can it be changed by any means at all? If so, how? And how should we assess the Gross National Happiness?

The early Utilitarians had recognized that implementing their programme required a device for measuring happiness—a hedonimeter. No such device exists, of course. We can ask people how happy they feel. This turns out to be a surprisingly revealing exercise, as we shall see. However, happiness has multiple senses. Its function in the sentence, 'I was happy to see Bob', may be rather different from that in the sentence, 'I was happy with the foreign policy of the government'. So before we could use judgements of happiness as a touchstone for public life, we would need to undertake a great deal of empirical work on people's thoughts and feelings about happiness, and how the feeling of happiness relates to the quality of life. This is work that psychologists have begun over the last few decades, and its illuminating results will be reviewed in this book.

In Chapter 1, we examine the concept of happiness and attempt to tease apart its various senses. Some varieties of happiness may be more measurable than others, and some, perhaps not the same ones, more worth pursuing. Chapter 2 examines the question of whether people are basically happy or basically unhappy, and why. Chapters 3 and 4 turn to the question of why some people seem to be happier than others: are people happy because good things happen to them, or do good things happen to them because they are happy? We shall see evidence that people's enduring levels of happiness come at least as much from themselves and the way they think as they do from the objective facts of their circumstances. Chapter 5 turns to the brain systems underlying emotions and moods. The feeling of well-being emerges from the interplay of neural circuits that are the products of millions of years of evolution. In men as in mice, positive and negative emotions rely on separate, dedicated neural circuits, which respond to status, to threats, and to rewards in the environment. The systems controlling pleasure are not identical to those controlling desire. This is an important lesson; the psychology of aspiration is not that of satisfaction. We do not always want what we like or like what we want.

Chapter 6 considers the problem of how to be happier, from the kinds of remedies on offer to the ways in which they can work. Finally, Chapter 7 attempts to synthesize briefly what we know about the often paradoxical psychology of happiness, and consider why we might be set up the way that we are. We are designed not for happiness or unhappiness, but to strive for the goals that evolution has built into us. Happiness is a handmaiden to evolution's purposes here, functioning not so much as an actual reward but as an imaginary goal that gives us direction and purpose. That goal may never get any nearer, but it may not need to. Jefferson's fundamental right, after all, was not happiness itself, but the pursuit of happiness. Nothing, not even a Utopia, can necessarily make the pursuit of happiness a successful one that ends in capture. The best society can merely allow every individual to flourish in the pursuit. And, looked at in the right way, this may be enough. The book concludes with a discussion of the prospects for future happiness. We, in the developed world at least, are wealthier, healthier, and freer than ever before. To expect large gains in happiness to follow suit may be unrealistic, for reasons which will become clear. There is even evidence that certain types of unhappiness are on the rise, and we will consider why this may be.

The problem with the concept of happiness is trying to make it do enough without making it do too much. If we define it narrowly as a certain type of feeling or physiological state, then we can, in principle, measure it objectively, but it is too trivial a thing to be the foundation of all public life and private decisions. On the other hand, if we define it broadly as something like 'the elements of the good life', then it is so broad as to beg the question, and certainly too broad to be measured in national statistics. Yet we intuitively feel that there *is* something called happiness, something unitary but not trivial, concrete enough to strive for yet broad enough to be worth striving for. The pursuit of this familiar, obscure, paradoxical object of desire is the theme of this book. The concept of happiness is a bit like a mirage to social scientists—it shimmers on the horizon as an appealing object of study, but often has a tendency to slip away when it is most closely approached. In this mirage-like quality, as we shall see, it is much like happiness itself.

1

Comfort and joy

At first glance, happiness seems a little like love: if you have to ask whether you are in it or not, you are probably not. Few of us much care to define it, but by heaven, we know it when we see it. The subjective, fuzzy, vague feel of the concept meant that happiness was neglected in psychology for many decades. For example, the 1985 *Penguin dictionary of psychology* moves unfalteringly from *haploid* to *haptic* without any signs of regret (*hedonic tone* gets three lines a few pages later). Surely, psychologists must have thought, happiness is a kind of homespun, folk category of thing that may have a certain use in bar-room gossip, but has no place in scholarly research articles. Actually, I will argue quite the opposite; however hard we try to fill our scholarly discourse with more palatable sounding alternatives (utility, hedonic tone, subjective well-being, positive emotionality), we are actually talking about some aspect of what gets agonized over in ordinary conversation. We do ourselves a disservice if we try to obfuscate this in neologisms. That doesn't mean that some conceptual tidying-up is out of place, though, as we shall see.

Early psychologists, like the reliably marvellous William James (1842–1910), brother of the novelist Henry James, had no doubt in their minds that psychology should be studied scientifically. However, they were also quite happy to take as the point of departure for the new science, everyday, folk psychological notions from their own lives, like love, happiness, faith, and so on. They are often misrepresented on this point as somehow knowing no better. The science of animal behaviour was in its infancy, so could not furnish a theoretical vocabulary to be borrowed for human psychology, and neuroscience scarcely existed. So they were before their time, stuck in some capacious armchair having to think about what people thought and felt until someone invented something better.

As soon as psychology could find ways of ditching armchair and bar-room notions, it did so. In the mid-twentieth century, psychologists were much more at home discussing rates of eye-blinking than love or joy. In time, eye-blinking evolved into more sophisticated behavioural measures like tiny differences in reaction times to given stimuli, but no one was much interested in connecting these up to big, messy, everyday notions like happiness. Indeed, the folk psychology of ordinary conversation, which trades in beliefs, desires, and feelings, was thought of by professionals as simply *bad psychology*, which stood to psychological truth roughly as painting someone blue and doing a dance around them at sunrise stands to antibiotics.

The truth, though, is that William James' desire to start from the notions of people's everyday thinking about psychology actually had a positive reason behind it. James seems to have understood that doing psychology is really like doing anthropology, and any anthropologist worth his malaria tablets begins by finding out what the people he is studying think it is that they do. It doesn't mean that they will turn out to be right, but how they think about their lives is an important part of the phenomenon under study.

Thus I would argue that if people spend a lot of their time thinking about the notion of happiness, then that is a pretty good reason for studying it. This is true whether or not they ever achieve it, and whether or not it can be given a water-tight definition. The ideas of happiness and its pursuit are part of the natural history of human beings, and so deserve their share of scientific attention.

Psychology has moved in this direction in an interesting way over the last few decades, and is probably closer to William James' concerns now than it was for most of the intervening years. In particular, the ways that people report what they think and feel about behaviour are now worthy objects of study. This is especially true with respect to the emotions and moods, and to happiness, as we shall see.

There are several reasons for the change. The work of Paul Ekman, starting in the 1960s, has been particularly important for research in the emotions. Before Ekman, emotions seemed precisely the kind of vague, subjective folk notions that psychologists avoided like the plague. Ekman, however, decided to start with some anthropology (in so doing, interestingly, he was reviving the neglected work of that near contemporary of William James, Charles Darwin). He took photographs of (American) actors displaying various emotions. He then asked participants to identify which emotion the expression went with. Unsurprisingly, American participants were pretty good at recognizing the emotions. However, Ekman also took these photographs and showed them to members of the Dani ethnic group in remote Papua New Guinea. By and large they agreed with the Americans about which face goes with which emotion.

These results have been replicated in many cultures. Ekman's work allowed the identification of a set of basic

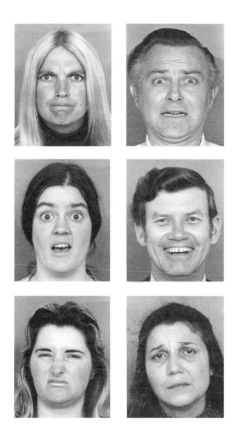

Fig. 1.1 Faces displaying basic emotions, used by Paul Ekman in his research. The emotions are anger, fear, surprise, joy, disgust, and sadness.

emotions—fear, sadness, disgust, anger, surprise, and joy—which are universally recognized. As well as agreeing which expression goes with which feeling, people across cultures agree which feeling goes with which situation. A snake in the picnic hamper, that's fear; the death by natural causes of a loved one, that's sadness; the contamination of the food you are eating by faeces, that's disgust; and the unexpected arrival of someone you love and miss terribly, that's joy. These emotions may be hard to define, but people from diverse cultures know them when they see them, and since they look like they come as standard features on your basic model *Homo sapiens*, we ought to find out how they work and what they are for. Interestingly, Ekman's work means that in the field of emotion research, the same notions that turn up in ordinary conversation also turn up in academic psychology papers.

Another important development has been the birth of evolutionary psychology. This influential perspective, which is very much in vogue at present, tries to explain features of the way our minds work with reference to the evolutionary challenges those minds were designed to solve. At some level evolutionary psychology has to be true. Every single one of our ancestors managed to stay alive until reproductive age, find a mate, and rear a child to adulthood. Most people throughout most of human history have not managed this, so our progenitors must have either had innately, or been able to learn, pretty smart ways of coping with the challenge. Of course, how much about the detail of how the mind works can be predicted from these truths is still something to be worked out.

The important thing about evolutionary psychology, though, is not that it says evolution has shaped everything we now do—it hasn't directly shaped mobile telephony or abstract expressionism—but that evolution has shaped the enduring ways we have for thinking about things. To take an example from leading evolutionary psychology theorists Leda Cosmides and John Tooby, again and again over evolutionary time, we faced the problem of a large carnivore running at speed towards us. Such a moment is really not the time to run through all possible subtleties of carnivore biology, the aesthetics of the big cat, or the relative merits of various responses to the situation. We want a ready-to-roll way of thinking—a software package that will start itself automatically when the cue comes—that has communication lines to key players like the heart and the legs already set up. None of our ancestors got eaten, so it is a fair bet that they were all running the best version of this particular programme. The programme—fear— might lead us to do things in modern life that are really stupid—for example, hiding under our seats whilst watching the film of *Jurassic park*—but having it has been advantageous over evolutionary time. The ways people become afraid today reflect the *design features* of the fear programme. (For example, people today are more afraid of Mad Cow epidemics and spiders than they are of electrical sockets and automobiles, which statistically is totally senseless. We are much more likely to be killed in an accident while driving during the course of one month than we are from eating infected beef in our entire lifetime. But there were food-transmitted epidemics and venomous spiders in Palaeolithic Africa, and no lunatics in Range Rovers.)

Evolutionary psychology thus makes it respectable to study the idea of happiness. Because people all over the world, and at different historical times, have thought about it, wanted it, debated it, maybe, like fear, it is a programme that is there for a reason. This will be the foundation of my argument in this book, though it turns out to be a little more complex. Joy certainly looks like a pre-specified programme in much the same way as fear. Happiness in its other senses is more complex. I will argue that what we are programmed for by evolution is not happiness itself, but a set of beliefs about the kinds of things that will bring happiness, and a disposition to pursue them. This makes sense of several consistent but puzzling findings: that people believe they will be more happy in the future than they are now, but in fact seldom are; that societies don't get happier as they get richer; and that people are consistently wrong about the impact of future life events on their happiness.

Ekman's work on emotions and evolutionary psychology are just two current trends that have joined what is now a broad flow of serious research on happiness. This movement has been known by various names, but the best is *hedonics*, the study of happiness (as opposed to *hedonism*, its pursuit). The seminal bibliography of hedonics contains more than 3000 studies published since 1960, and there has been, since 2000, a trade journal, the *Journal of happiness studies*. The members of this broad research effort include brain scientists, clinicians interested in preventing depression, social scientists interested in measuring human development in different countries, and economists interested in explaining people's consumption choices. It is an impressively interdisciplinary effort, since happiness is hard to pin down within any narrow set of concerns. Happiness is now returning to the central position in the human sciences that Jeremy Bentham assumed it would take.

*

This groundwork done; what, then, is happiness? The concept is slippery, but this does not negate its value. Happiness belongs to that class of concepts of which all the specific examples are related, like members of a family. That is to say, they all have something in common, but there is no one thing that shows up in all of them and in nothing else. The notion of happiness, helpfully for us, shows up in culture after culture. Many languages draw the distinction between something very immediate like *joy* or *pleasure*, and something more lasting and considered, like *satisfaction* or *contentment* (e.g. Italian *gioa* versus *felicità*). Note that whilst there might be quite a lot of *gioa* involved in a state of *felicita*, you would not have to be joyful all the time for the longer state to count as a happy one. In some languages, there is a specific lexical link between *happiness* and *good luck* (German *Gluck/glucklich* happy/lucky; *good hap* in English originally meant good luck). This suggests that something in the happiness family is to do with things turning out better than it was reasonable to expect. Thus, being happy might not always be an absolute state, but contains implicit comparison with an expectation or with what other people have.

These observations are sufficient to allow us to begin to sketch the semantic terrain of happiness. Most usages of the term can be classified into one of three increasingly inclusive senses (Fig. 1.2). The most immediate and direct senses of happiness involve an emotion or feeling, something like joy or pleasure. These feelings are transient and have an unmistakable and particular phenomenology—that is to say, paraphrasing Thomas Nagel, there is something which joy feels like. The feeling is brought on by a desired state being (perhaps unexpectedly) attained, and there is not much cognition involved, beyond the recognition that the desired thing has happened. With apologies for the barbaric terminology, we will henceforth call this sense of happiness 'level one happiness'.

When people say that they are happy with their lives, they do not usually mean that they are literally joyful, or experiencing pleasure, all of the time. They mean that, upon reflection on the balance sheet of pleasures and pains, they feel the balance to be reasonably positive over the long term. This is happiness in the sense usually studied by psychologists. It concerns not so much feelings, as judgements about the balance of feelings. Thus it is a hybrid of emotion, and judgement about emotion. Its synonyms are things like contentment and life satisfaction. This is 'level two happiness'. It is clear that when Bentham talked about the greatest happiness to the greatest number being the foundation of morals and legislation, he meant happiness in a level two

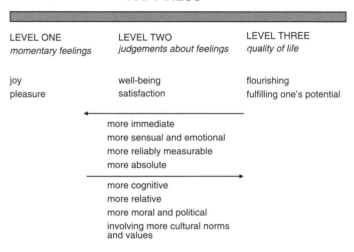

HAPPINESS

LEVEL ONE	LEVEL TWO	LEVEL THREE
momentary feelings	*judgements about feelings*	*quality of life*
joy	well-being	flourishing
pleasure	satisfaction	fulfilling one's potential

← more immediate
more sensual and emotional
more reliably measurable
more absolute

more cognitive →
more relative
more moral and political
involving more cultural norms and values

Fig. 1.2 Three different senses of the term 'happiness'. Each level includes the content of the level below, plus some additional things.

sense; the long-term balance of positive and negative emotions across time and individuals.

Level two happiness, though, is not calculated by a simple summing up of all the positive moments and a subtraction of the negative ones. It also involves more complex cognitive processes, such as comparison with alternative possible outcomes. Thus I could say, 'I am happy about how the first draft of my book came out', in the full knowledge that the first draft is dreadful. If I always write dreadful first drafts, but find it easier to revise them into good shape than I do to get the text down onto the page initially, then this makes perfect sense. I could be happy relative to my expectation that it would be awful, and my belief that the hard work is done by that point. Or, to take another example, if I usually cut myself shaving twice a day, then I could be happy to have cut myself just once today. However, it is unlikely that I took pleasure from the cut. The cut was a painful event which made me swear; the happiness stems from the subsequent processes that compared the pain I went through with the pain I expected or had experienced yesterday.

There are yet broader senses of happiness. Aristotle's ideal of the good life, *eudaimonia*, is sometimes translated as 'happiness'. However, what is meant by *eudaimonia* is a life in which the person flourishes, or fulfils their true potential. Though such a life *could* include many positive emotional experiences, it is not actually part of its definition that it need do so. Contemporary psychologists and philosophers have sometimes talked of happiness when they really mean the good life or *eudaimonia*. When they do so, we shall call this usage a level three sense of the term happiness. Note that 'level three happiness' has no characteristic phenomenology since it is not an emotional state. There is no single thing that it feels like to achieve *eudaimonia*, since everyone's potential is different. Indeed, one of the problems of *eudaimonia* and related constructs is that it is not clear who is to be the judge of what one's full potential is. If the judge is the subject herself then the concept is a properly psychological one, and useful in our discussion of happiness. If the judge is a psychologist, or society, imposing some external standard of what one should do with life, then the concept has become a moralizing one; an ideology, in fact. But, at least within any liberal tradition of thought, happiness should not be moralized. As long as people do not harm each other, then it is their inalienable right to construe their own potential in any way they like. To find a definition of happiness that is broad enough to capture the full range of human goods, but does not become an ideological position, is an extremely hard balance to strike, as we shall see.

In addition to the three levels of the ordinary meaning of happiness shown in Fig. 1.2, some scholars have used the term simply to mean the attainment of whatever it is that people want. This is particularly evident in economics. Jeremy Bentham and the classical economists hypothesized that people make their choices in life so as to maximize their happiness, or, as it was called, utility. By utility, they meant happiness in a level two sense. That is, they believed that if you had a pleasure-measuring device, then you would be able to show that the choices people made were the ones that maximized the balance of pleasurable feelings over painful ones. However, the lack of any practical way of measuring happiness or utility meant that, over time, economists took the utility of an outcome simply to mean the propensity of people to choose it. For example, if people prefer to spend money on cars rather than boats, then economists say that having a car gives greater utility than having boats. This is not a psychological hypothesis. Indeed, it is not an explanatory claim at all. The greater utility of cars cannot explain why people choose them, since the greater utility of cars is *defined* as the propensity of people to choose them. The concept is therefore merely a shorthand for a device for predicting people's behaviour when allocating scarce resources.

Sometimes, then, you will find arguments that take the following form: if people choose, for example, a higher income over more leisure time, it follows that a higher income must make people happier than more leisure time, otherwise they would not have chosen it. Here 'happiness' is being used to mean behavioural preference. It says nothing about the actual emotional content of the two outcomes. It merely describes people's propensity to choose one or the other. This usage is quite different from that of ordinary language. There are all kinds of reasons that people might choose A over B without A making them happier than B (for example, because they wrongly estimate how much they will enjoy A, because they feel morally obligated, because everyone else around them is choosing A, and so on).

Which definition of happiness we adopt makes a real difference to what we can do and what we conclude. For one thing, the different level definitions are more or less amenable to scientific study. Level one happiness can, in principle, be measured objectively. We might well discover a physiological mechanism or brain region that is dedicated to pleasure (see Chapter 5), and be able to measure its activity. At the very least, in level one terms, people's subjective report of their happiness is king. If they say they are experiencing joy, then we have to take it that they are, and we can record this response as a data point. The same is true to a lesser extent with level two happiness. Here, the different standards of comparison that different individuals employ in their judgements could become a confounding factor, but people's self-reports of happiness are still the primary and proper data points for a scientific study.

Happiness level three is not something that can be so easily measured. As we have seen, assessing it involves making a judgement about what the good life consists of and the extent to which one's life fulfils it. The psychologist Carol Ryff and colleagues have argued that human well-being involves a broader suite of elements than just level two happiness. This suite includes personal growth, purpose, mastery of one's environment, and self-directness, as well as the more familiar elements of pleasure and lack of pain. The broader components of Ryff's concept of psychological well-being tend to be correlated with narrower happiness, but the correlations are quite weak, which means that you can find individuals high on psychological well-being, and low on level two happiness, and vice versa.

Ryff's research is convincing, but in its presentation there can be confusion between a psychological conception of well-being and a moral position. For example, Ryff states that 'history provides countless examples of those who lived ugly, unjust, or pointless lives who were nonetheless happy'. The implication is that level two happiness *per se* is a reprehensibly narrow goal to pursue if done at the cost of beauty or purpose. Indeed, since things like beauty and purpose are rather difficult and challenging, we should generally take a cut in short-term happiness to pursue them. But if someone's life is, to my mind, ugly or pointless but they nonetheless enjoy it, it is hard to see what right I have to suggest that they should be doing something else. In doing so, I would unavoidably be bringing an evaluative agenda of my own to bear, and so would have left the domain of objective science for a kind of tyranny of experts. A person is pretty lucky if they really enjoy life, and the last thing they need is to be chastised for their narrowness or exhorted by privileged academics to struggle to write novels. On the other hand, Ryff is right that, for many people, level two happiness is not a be all and end all.

Ryff is careful to stress that the broader 'psychological well-being' that she studies should not be referred to as 'happiness'. Others are not so careful with terminology. This is particularly true in the movement known as Positive Psychology. Positive Psychology has arisen in the last few years, mainly in North America, as a self-conscious antidote to psychology's traditional emphasis on disorders, failings, and weaknesses—depression, anxiety, addiction, and so on. Why should there not be a systematic framework for studying strengths and resources, like happiness, courage, purpose, and good cheer? Positive Psychology is an interesting hybrid in that it attempts to combine the methodological rigour of academic psychology with a willingness to prescribe that is usually restricted to the self-help section of the bookshop.

For example, there has been much interest within Positive Psychology in the state known as *flow*. This state is characterized by total absorption in a challenging activity for which the individual has the skills, albeit the skills are stretched to their limits. Rock climbers, musicians, and athletes enter the state of flow relatively often, but there are innumerable ways of doing so, and we could all find ways of getting more flow into our lives. Other prescriptions of Positive Psychology are finding meaning, spirituality, and higher purpose in life. Perhaps the *summum bonum* as far as Positive Psychology is concerned is developing the *autotelic personality*. An autotelic person:

Needs few material possessions and little entertainment, comfort, power or fame, because so much of what he or she does is already rewarding ... they are less dependent on external rewards that keep others motivated to go on with a life composed of dull and meaningless routines. They are more autonomous and independent, because they cannot be as easily manipulated with threats or rewards from the outside. At the same time, they are more involved with everything around them because they are fully immersed in the current of life.

Now I can easily be persuaded that flow, purpose, and an autotelic personality might be good things to pursue (even if this version of the autotelic life sounds like nothing so much as a non-conformist Protestant who happens to be independently wealthy). What is interesting is that none of these things have much to do with happiness in the ordinary sense. People with a lot of flow in their lives are less bored and apathetic than others, but they score absolutely no higher in their responses to questions about how happy they are. Indeed, they must be disposed to be pretty unhappy or they would probably be content with the 'dull and meaningless routines' that their brethren seem to put up with. Studies of high-flow professions such as musicians, artists, and writers show that these individuals are prone to deep dissatisfaction, which moves them forward in their quest, as well as bouts of depression and addiction. By contrast, studies of people who are very happy in the level two sense show that, far from being 'autonomous and independent', they are compulsively social extroverts.

There is an ambiguity about whether the prescription to seek the autotelic life is a piece of advice on how to feel better, or a moral position. Mihalyi Csikszentmilhalyi, in his classic work on the subject, seems to moralize it:

> Other things being equal, a life filled with complex flow activities is more worth living than one spent consuming passive entertainment.

The judgement that one person's life is more worth living than another person's is a very problematic one. Especially since, as Csikszentmilhalyi is careful to make clear, the flow-filled life is not a *happier* one than the one spent consuming passive entertainment. His book-jacket writer is not so careful, however, as the back blurb says: 'Csikszentmilhalyi argues that human beings are at their most creative, most rewarded *and happiest* when they are performing in a state of flow ... ' (my emphasis).

A similar tension exists in Martin Seligman's *Authentic*

happiness, the book that in many ways defines Positive Psychology. Despite the title, much of the book is not about increasing happiness in a level two sense. Seligman believes that people's experience of positive emotion is at least partly limited by their temperament, and that pleasure is so subject to habituation that it is unreliable as a source of the good life. Thus we should instead seek a diffcrent set of goods—gratification, flow, wisdom, justice, spirituality, and so on, not because they necessarily bring positive emotions, but because they are intrinsically worthwhile. This is a conclusion that can hardly be disagreed with. However, it is odd to argue that a set of goods which are distinct from happiness and do not depend upon happiness for their value should be considered crucial elements of 'authentic happiness'. Seligman tries to clarify this argument with a definition of his terms:

> I use *happiness* and *well-being* as overarching terms to describe the goals of the whole positive psychology enterprise, embracing both positive feelings ... and positive activities that have no feeling component at all . . . . It is important to recognize that 'happiness' and 'well-being' sometimes refer to feelings, but sometimes refer to activities in which nothing at all is felt.

Though Seligman is right to point out that there is

more to life than happiness, he muddies the waters with his definition. What he has offered is a level three definition of happiness, wherein happiness includes a whole portfolio of human goods. But this departs from the ordinary language sense of the word. Would people picking up *Authentic happiness* in a book shop really have expected the condition described therein to be one 'with no feeling component'? They would not, since our intuitive definition of happiness includes our feelings about things as its core. And if happiness is defined to include activities that don't make the actor feel good, who is to be the arbiter of whether they are 'positive' or not? It looks like an evaluative moral framework is being smuggled in strapped to the underbelly of psychological science.

Several tentative conclusions can thus be reached. When people talk of happiness, they generally mean a state involving positive feelings or positive judgements about feelings. These—level one and level two—senses of happiness will be the focus in the rest of this book. When the definition is made any broader, to include other human values and goods, the concept becomes incoherent. The flip side of this is that there are other important human goods which are not reducible to happiness in this sense. That is the valid point that Ryff, Seligman, and Csikszentmilhalyi all make. Nor should the assumption be made that whatever it is people have chosen is that which makes them happiest.

A second point to emerge is that people are really fascinated by happiness and, in particular, any way of increasing it. This is presumably why Csikszentmilhalyi's jacket editor slips the term 'happiness' in to sell a book on flow, and Seligman calls his book *Authentic happiness*, not *The good life*. The former sounds appealing, and the latter worthy. Perhaps this reflects the individualistic ethos of our culture, with its focus on personal pleasure, or perhaps it suggests an important universal feature of our psychology of emotion, as I shall argue in later chapters.

Happiness is universally thought of as a positive condition, and this is particularly true of the level one joy or pleasure sense of happiness. There are some interesting contrasts between the negative and the positive emotions. To paraphrase Tolstoy, every positive emotion is alike, but every negative emotion is negative in its own way. That is, each of the negative emotions comes with a particular schema about what type of problem is occurring, and what a favoured solution might be. Consider the examples in Table 1.1. Each negative emotion is evoked by a particular situation type or schema, and each one potentiates a

Table 1 The four main negative emotions, the situation types that evoke them, and the kinds of remedies that they suggest.

Emotion	Schema	Remedy
Fear	Ongoing source of danger	Detect and flee
Anger	Violation of norm or agreement by other person	Deter future violation e.g. by punch on the nose, letter to *The Times*, etc.
Sadness	Loss of valued support	Save energy and tread carefully until conditions improve
Disgust	Potential contamination	Spit it out and avoid

particular class of remedy to make that schema go away.

The function of each emotion programme is highly specific and totally different from the others. All the negative emotions say, 'something bad has happened' but they disagree about what remedy to take. That is why we have several different negative emotions—note that of Ekman's basic six, four are negative and only one positive—that feel so categorically distinct from each other.

Joy, on the other hand says, 'something good has happened'. Its prescription for the appropriate remedy is simply 'don't change anything'. Though the sources and intensities of joy may vary, they all belong to the same spectrum. This is because there is only one way of going about not changing anything. Thus, we can see happiness/joy as a programme for detecting changes in the environment that are good for us, putting other concerns and intentions aside to allow us to focus on the good thing. (To test this hypothesis, try going back to your routine work when your heart is full of joy about some recent good news. Difficult, isn't it?).

Other asymmetries between the positive and negative emotional states follow from this. The negative emotions can be very persistent. It is possible to imagine living in chronic fear, if the sources of fear are not remedied. On the other hand, you might be joyful when a long-lost cousin arrives, but you can't imagine remaining joyful for as long as he stays. The joy gradually ebbs away, even if the bringer of that joy is still present. If the joy programme is there to divert other concerns in order to allow us to concentrate on something good, then it would be pretty dysfunctional if it didn't have a built in shut-down mechanism after a while. Sooner or later we get hungry or tired, or need to avoid a predator, so well-designed joy should gradually

move into the background and allow other pro-
grammes to capture attention. Habituation happens
with the negative emotions, too, but less quickly and
completely.

The sources of joy are quite varied. One recent
study identified the main ones as interactions with
friends, food, drink, and sex, and the experience of
success in some domain. From an evolutionary
psychology perspective, it is easy to characterize these
as the type of events that would lead to increased fitness in ancestral environments, and to which it would
be worth temporarily diverting other concerns to
allocate time to.

It would be exhausting to spend all of your waking
life full of joy, besides which it could probably only be
done with access to a chemistry lab and a great deal of
money. Most of us understand that the big issue in life is
not being joyful, which is at best going to be an occa-
sional perk, but being happy in the sense of generally
satisfied overall. Most psychological research, and
almost all of the rest of this book, will concern level two
happiness, which psychologists call *subjective well-being*. A
key component of subjective well-being is *life satisfaction*.
This is the kind of feeling that is tapped when you
answer questions like: 'Taking things overall, how happy

are you with life in general?' or 'How satisfied are you with your life overall?'

The answers to these questions correlate highly with that to the question 'How happy do you generally feel?' With joy, it is plausible that people can look directly inside themselves and perceive how much of it they are undergoing. With satisfaction, it is clear that self-reports are related to emotions that people experience, but via an indirect, cognitive process, usually involving some kind of comparison. That is why a natural response to, 'How satisfied do you feel?' is, 'With what, and what are the alternatives?' It may also explain why self-reports of life satisfaction are notoriously sensitive to context.

For example, in one study, experimenters contrived to allow participants to find a dime on the photocopy machine just before they were asked questions about life satisfaction. Participants who had just found a dime reported significantly higher satisfaction *with their entire lives*. That has to be the cheapest and most effective public policy measure imaginable.

Unfortunately, it wouldn't work if everyone expected a dime when they went to make a copy. The positive emotion arose because things went better than expected in a particular domain (remember the link between happiness and luck). The question about life satisfaction lacked a very specific frame of reference, so presumably the participants sampled their emotional state, found the small joy of the dime still there, and so inferred that life was going pretty well. You can get many other similar effects; ask people on a sunny day, or after something good has just happened, or even in a nice room, and they will say that they are a little more satisfied with life than if the context is less pleasant. And the opposite effect is real and dangerous; talk to someone who has just had a set-back in one particular domain, and they will tell you that nothing ever works out for them, and that life in general is going badly.

Thus, one source of people's judgement about life satisfaction is the mood they are in. More specifically, people will use their current mood unless there is evidence that this is not a good cue to how satisfied they are. In a nice study that showed this clearly, Norbert Schwarz and colleagues telephoned people on sunny or rainy days to ask them about life satisfaction. As predicted, on sunny days people reported higher satisfaction, *unless* the experimenter drew attention to the weather, for example by saying 'How's the weather down there?' Once the weather had been mentioned, people realized that it was a plausible reason for their current mood, which they then adjusted by an appropriate amount in judging their overall satisfaction. This kind of effect has good uses in psychotherapy;

a person might be inclined to feel that nothing in their entire life is going well, but the therapist can draw attention to the fact that the patient has only had a setback in one particular domain, and that his current negative mood is completely explicable by that, not by the quality of his life in general.

One influential view of the relationship between satisfaction (level two happiness) and emotional experience (level one happiness) is that satisfaction is the balance of negative and positive emotions experienced in life—the balance, in other words, of pleasures and pains. You might think, by the way, that the amount of negative emotion and the amount of positive emotion in life ought to be inversely related, so that as one increases, the other decreases. This is not in fact so. Whilst it is hard to have negative and positive emotions at the same moment, over the run of life, you can have frequent negative emotions and frequent positive emotions, or alternately, infrequent positive and infrequent negative ones. Some people experience more emotional ups *and* downs than others, so that when we correlate the frequencies of positive and negative emotions across a group of people, we find essentially no relationship.

An ideal measure of satisfaction would be the balance of pleasures and pains experienced, but when people are asked to judge their own satisfaction, what they do is clearly different from this simple subtraction. For example, in one study people were asked to think about three negative or three positive events that had happened in their lives. In one condition, the events had to be recent, whereas in the other they had to be events from five years ago. They were then asked about their overall life satisfaction.

What happened was that those considering negative recent events reported lower satisfaction than those considering positive recent events. But those considering negative distant events reported themselves as happier than those considering positive distant events. The interpretation of this result is all to do with frame of reference. Those considering recent events included them in their summary of how life was going now, and so positive ones made them happier and negative ones more gloomy. Those considering past events used them as a *comparison* with how their life was now. Therefore considering only positive events from the past was bound to make the present a bit disappointing, but consider some awful things from the past, and suddenly the present looks like an improvement.

At other times, the frame of reference can be someone else's life, or what might have been. In one famous study, people were asked how satisfied they were with their partner either before or after being shown photographs of models. Predictably, especially for men, the availability (at least in the imagination) of the models lowered their satisfaction with their real partners. Olympic bronze medallists report higher satisfaction than silver medallists. For them, the natural comparison is with not getting a medal at all, which they narrowly escaped. For the silver winners, the natural comparison is the gold, which they missed out on.

Where we think we are in the pile can be a powerful determinant of how we feel about life. As H. L. Mencken observed, a wealthy man is one who earns $100 more than his wife's sister's husband. A majority of people, when asked, would prefer to earn $50,000 in a world where others earned $25,000, than $100,000 in a world where others earned $250,000. Moreover, people's assessment of the minimum amount that it would be possible to live on rises year on year in line with increases in wages, not rises in prices.

The fear programme is obviously designed to get us away from things that are likely to harm us. If we had to make an analogous claim about the purpose of the happiness system, we would be most likely to say that it is there to keep us moving towards things that are likely to be good for us in some appropriate biological sense—mating, good food, pleasant environments—and away from things that are bad for us. It is like a metal detector dial that increases its bleeping when we get close to something valuable, and makes increasingly unpleasant noises as we move away from areas likely to contain treasure. Thus, we make decisions about what to do in life based on the reading from the metal detector.

Now, if happiness worked in this way, we would expect there to be certain capacities built into the system. We should accurately remember how good or bad past experiences made us feel. This is so we know whether to avoid them again in the future. We should also be good predictors of how much more or less happy we will feel if we make particular choices out of the alternatives available to us.

Interestingly, neither of these conditions seem to be fulfilled. Several studies have shown that people overestimate the extent to which life changes will affect their happiness, for good or bad. Most famously, winners of tens of thousands of pounds in lotteries are no more happy than the general population, and the return to normal happiness levels takes only a very few months. Effects like these are due to the phenomenon of adaptation, which means we re-centre ourselves around the new situation, a phenomenon which we will explore further in a subsequent chapter. Importantly, when we think about our future happiness we often fail to predict our own adaptation. One side-effect of adaptation is the so-called endowment effect, where we think it would be really hard to get along without something we now have, forgetting that we got along quite fine without it for years.

The endowment effect is really easy to elicit. For example, participants were given a choice between a mug and a sum of money, and asked to indicate how much the sum would have to be for them to prefer the cash. The sum was about $3.50 on average. Alternatively, participants were given a mug for keeps. They were then asked how much money they would accept to give up the mug. Now they said they would need on average $7.12. The two conditions used identical mugs. Yet, in as much as money is an indicator of utility, the participants seemed to believe that the mug was improving their lives by over twice as much in the case where it was already theirs.

So much for our ability to make choices on the basis of the happiness that things yield. What about past happiness? When remembering how good or bad a past experience felt, our judgements seem to be based largely on the average of two factors: how good or bad the peak moment was, and how good or bad the end was. The total amount of pleasure or pain experienced is often neglected. This effect is clear in a study by Nobel-prize-winning behavioural scientist Daniel Kahneman and his colleagues. Participants had the reliably unpleasant task of plunging one of their hands into cold water and keeping it there. In one condition, the trial lasted 60 seconds, and the water was at 14°C. In the other condition, after 60 seconds at 14°C, the water was warmed to 15°C for a further 30 seconds before the participant could take his hand out. A few minutes later, when given the choice of which of the trials to repeat, the majority of the participants chose the long one!

Note that (a) having your hand in cold water is very unpleasant, (b) it gets worse as it goes on, and (c) 15°C is still cold. So why were the participants choosing the trial with the greater amount of pain? In both trials, the peak moment was equally bad (14°C). In the long one, however, the ending was slightly less bad, and therefore the average of the peak and the ending was slightly more favourable. But the fact remains that the people were choosing more pain over less. In a related clinical study, Kahneman's group showed that patients preferred a colonscopy which was really painful for a short time, and then just fairly painful for a while longer, over one which was really painful for a short time and then stopped. The implication of this rule for happiness is that we might often be tempted to fall for things that provide either a high peak of joy or remain joyful right to the end, when in fact we would maximize the amount of pleasure in our lives if we chose things that went on for longer at a lower level of intensity. The former type of thing—a big night out, for example—might make a greater psychological impact in terms of the average of peak and end, but the latter—a good weighty novel, or a new skill acquired—might provide more lasting happiness if all its moments were added up.

Kahneman uses results such as these to draw a distinction between objective and subjective happiness. This seems like a strange distinction to draw, when all happiness is intrinsically about subjective experience. However, what Kahneman means is that level one experiences provide a kind of raw data of happiness, namely how good or bad we feel from moment to moment. If we want to make a level two judgement of how happy we have been, we should simply sum up this level one data, which we could in principle collect by having a meter running in our pocket that we flipped every time we made a transition between feeling good and feeling bad (a hedonimeter!) The meter would provide an objective summary of our subjective experience.

What we actually do when we try to consider how

happy we are, have been, or will be, is something much cruder than the objective summary of level one experiences. We make a kind of best guess, or subjective estimate of our subjective experience. The guess is biased by things like the peak-end rule, our current mood, the standard of comparison we are making, and our failure to predict our own adaptation. This means we may end up with an inaccurate picture of the net effects of our behaviour on our happiness, and choose things that don't in fact make us happier. I will argue later in the book that these effects are probably not faults in the happiness programme; they are the way that it is designed. That is, the purpose of the happiness programme in the human mind is not to increase human happiness; it is to keep us striving. That is why it tells us so clearly that if we just had a £30,000 salary, we would be much happier than we are now on £20,000, but as soon as we achieve that goal, whispers that perhaps it was actually closer to £40,000 that is really needed to guarantee lasting bliss.

The effects we have seen in this chapter—particularly comparison and adaptation—have huge implications for happiness, as well as hedonics. They mean that when people tell us how happy they are, we may be partly picking up the psychological framing of the question rather than the objective circumstances of their lives. They also mean that great unhappiness in life is often a result of thinking about things in the wrong way rather than objective circumstances; failing to discount other reasons for moods, making the wrong comparisons, or dwelling on the past in the wrong way. They also raise questions that we have to confront as a society. For example, what does it mean for our satisfaction with our lives that the magazines on every news stand are full of airbrushed images of lipo-sucked supermodels, and tales of men who ski off glaciers with world leaders, and list their hobbies as judo, chess, and the *Kama Sutra* (in the original Sanskrit, of course)? With all these questions in mind, we will now turn to survey evidence about how happy people actually are.

2

Bread and circuses

'If the immediate purpose of our existence is not suffering, then our existence is the most ill-adapted to its purpose in the world', wrote Arthur Schopenhauer in a late essay entitled *On the suffering of the world*. Misfortune and unhappiness, he argues, are the rule rather than the exception in life: 'Work, worry, toil and trouble are indeed the lot of almost all men their whole life long.'

It is true that human beings often have a great deal to worry about, from financial uncertainty, to poor health, to unrequited love, to the disappointment of not realizing life-long dreams. And Schopenhauer certainly has some very interesting insights into the logic of happiness. However, here, he is making an empirical claim; that is, that most people are generally pretty unhappy.

Schopenhauer stands at the head of a line of great European thinkers and artists who were *happiness pessimists* (Fig. 2.1). That is, they believed that the conditions necessary for happiness are extremely hard to attain, usually because of some profound gap between what we want and what we can actually have. For example, the knowledge of our own death, society's repression of our drives, or the cruel and illusory psychology of desire, put us in a state of eternal angst. The world the pessimists described was one in which most people are basically unhappy, and will remain so either forever, or until some kind of unlikely utopia can be constructed (which may take even longer).

An alternative hypothesis is the contention that most people, by and large, are satisfied with their lot. As Roman satirist Juvenal wrote: 'the public has long since cast off its cares . . . and longs eagerly for just two things: bread and circuses!' Now Juvenal was generally a happiness pessimist, believing like the good Stoic he was that people were often made miserable by the vanity of their own desires. In this particular passage, though, he is apparently making the opposite claim; that if asked, most people whose basic needs for sustenance and minimal entertainment are met would say that they were happy.

We might call these two positions the *Sturm und Drang hypothesis* ('want and boredom are . . . the twin poles of human life') and the *bread and circuses hypothesis* ('the public has long since cast off its cares'). If we take them

Fig. 2.1 Grumpy old men: Larkin, Freud, Nietzsche, Sartre, Schopenhauer, Wittgenstein. Many great European intellectuals have been happiness pessimists. Match the quotations with the photographs. (Answers in the notes at the back.)

Quotations:

1 One feels inclined to say that the intention that man should be happy is not included in the plan of Creation.

2 The existentialist says at once that man is in anguish.

3 Throughout the ages the wisest of men have passed the same judgement of life: it is no good.

4 I don't know why we are here, but I'm pretty sure that it is not in order to enjoy ourselves.

5 Today it is bad, and day by day it will get worse—until at last the worst of all arrives.

6 Man hands on misery to man/It deepens like a coastal shelf/Get out as early as you can/And don't have any kids yourself.

as descriptive hypotheses (that is, ideas about how the world is, not how it should be), then it becomes a simple empirical matter to find out which one is right.

The UK periodically carries out large-scale studies of a cross-section of its population. For example, in what is known as the National Child Development Study (NCDS), all the children born between March 3rd and March 9th 1958 were studied extensively. Every detail about their births, family backgrounds, school attainment, and health has been recorded from 1958 to the present (they are now in their forties). Every few years, those that can be traced have been interviewed about many aspects of their lives. The archives of the NCDS now contain literally thousands of data on each of the cohort members, and thus it offers a unique picture of how a whole slice of the population develops, thinks, and behaves. As well as allowing researchers to answer questions about themes specific to the UK in this particular historical epoch, the breadth and detail of the data mean that universal questions about topics like health, marriage, and happiness can be investigated. The results confirm and expand what we know from many smaller studies from different parts of the world.

The NCDS participants have often been asked questions relating to happiness. For example, in 2000, at the

mid-life crisis peak age of 42, they were asked to indicate their satisfaction with how their lives had turned
out so far, on a scale of 1 to 10. The results are stunning
(Fig. 2.2). More than 90% of the 11,269 respondents
chose 5 or above. More than half of them chose 8, 9, or
10, with 8 the most frequent choice overall.

These results are very much in keeping with those of
dozens of other surveys in many different countries.
When asked, most people say that they are happy or
very happy, and this result is robust as regards age,
place, sex, or different ways of asking the question.
Just as in Lake Wobegon, pretty much everyone claims
above average levels of satisfaction with their lives. As a
description of the general condition of the populace,
the Sturm und Drang hypothesis doesn't really get past
first base.

Of course, the studies I have quoted, and most psychological investigations, are carried out in extremely
affluent populations, where many of the pains and fears
that must have loomed large in historical times have
been brought under control. Perhaps if we were to survey a population that lacked modern luxury, we would
find more evidence of human misery.

There are by now several large international comparison studies, and interestingly there are significant
differences between nations. We will turn to these in

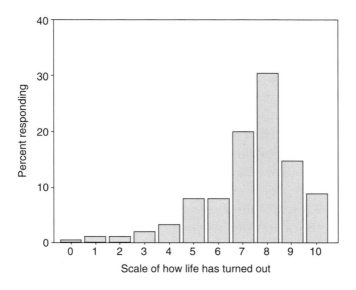

Fig. 2.2 Distribution of responses to the question of how life has turned out, on a scale of 1 to 10, from the 2000 sweep of the National Child Development Study.

the next chapter, but here it is worthy of note that the tendency is still towards the positive. In none of 42 countries surveyed in the early 1990s, for example, is the average as low as 5.0, the mid-point on a ten-point scale (Table 2.1). The spectrum goes from the lugubrious Bulgarians with an average satisfaction of 5.03, to the positively nauseating Swiss with an average of 8.39 (which means either very few people are discontented, or some people were giving answers higher than 10). It is also worthy of note that all the averages lower than 6 are countries which had just undergone the rapid transition from communism. This destabilization was

Table 2.1 Average life satisfaction (on a ten point scale) for a large sample of individuals from a selection of countries.

Bulgaria	5.03	Italy	7.24
Russia	5.37	Argentina	7.25
Romania	5.88	Brazil	7.39
Hungary	6.03	Mexico	7.41
India	6.21	United Kingdom	7.48
Czech Republic	6.4	Chile	7.55
Nigeria	6.4	Finland	7.68
Japan	6.53	United States	7.71
South Korea	6.69	Ireland	7.87
France	6.76	Sweden	8.02
China	7.05	Denmark	8.16
Spain	7.13	Switzerland	8.39

bound to make everyone apprehensive about life for a time. Among countries with more stable conditions, even very poor countries, turned in averages quite closely bunched in the 6–8 range (India, 6.21; Nigeria, 6.40; China, 7.05).

Why are people so happy? Is it simply that positive emotions are more frequent in life than negative ones, and so the balance is in the black? This may be true, but there are also other reasons people might report better-than-middling happiness when asked. Chronic unhappiness might indicate perceived failure to achieve life goals, or unfavourable comparisons with the achievement of others. As well as being things to avoid for their own sake, these are, to paraphrase evolutionary psychologist, Geoffrey Miller, things you might not want to admit to on a first date. That is, unhappiness is not just unfortunate; it is unattractive in a potential mate, friend, or colleague. This effect was pointed out by Adam Smith, father of free-market economics, who was an accomplished theoretician of emotions:

> Nothing is more graceful than habitual cheerfulness.
> . . . It is quite otherwise with grief . . . the man who is made uneasy by every little disagreeable incident . . . will seldom meet with much sympathy.

Thus, one reason for such high self-reported happiness is that people are aware of the signals they are giving off and so they *impression manage*. Some indication that this effect is significant comes from the finding that people report higher levels of well-being in face-to-face interviews than in postal surveys. This effect is particularly pronounced when the interviewer is of the opposite sex. It is easy to understand the temptation to do this. (It is also worth remembering when you feel down, that if everyone seems happier than you are, that may only mean that they are good at seeming happy.)

As it turns out, there are many domains where most people think themselves above average. Most people believe that they are better than average drivers, above average on desirable personality traits like conscientiousness and kindness, and more likely than average to achieve future life goals. Obviously they cannot all be right! Part of these self-enhancement effects may be due to impression management. However, there could also be deeper reasons. The truth is that we go through the world in a considerable state of uncertainty. For example, it is really hard to get any kind of decent estimate of what the odds are of achieving some major life goal like a happy marriage or a place on the board. Given that we don't know what the odds are, we need to base our behaviour on a guess. A low guess would lead to passivity, for why try if the odds are unfavourable? A high guess would lead to striving, and even though that striving might often lead to failure, sometimes it would lead to success. In other words, since we don't *know* what the outcome of life will be, it might be better to behave *as if* we can get what we want if we try hard enough. If this theory is correct, it would predict that self-enhancement would appear wherever the benefits of success are much greater than the costs of trying and failing. It also predicts that in domains where the costs of trying and failing are very high, self-enhancement should be replaced by caution. This is a prediction psychologists are trying to test at the moment.

These effects are relevant to happiness judgements in the following way. The question 'How happy are you in general?' put baldly, lacks any appropriate frame of reference, so people seek one, probably by comparing themselves either to peers or to some ideal of what they want. If they have a rose-tinted view of where they stand relative to their peers, and how easy it will be to attain what they want, then of course they will come up with the inference that they must be pretty happy. Thus the finding that most people are pretty happy is in part a reflection of the endearingly unrealistic psychology with which we address the world, a conclusion that both

Juvenal and Schopenhauer would have been pleased with.

If most people say that they are happy, does that mean that most of us are living in the best of all possible worlds? In the NCDS, though most people were pretty satisfied, fewer than 10% of respondents gave themselves a perfect 10. The NCDS researchers also asked the cohort members where, on the same scale of 1 to 10, they thought their life would be in ten-years time. The results are illuminating. You will recall that the average satisfaction with life now was 7.39. Well, the average of where people thought they would be in ten-years time was 8.05. Only 5% thought they would be at a worse position in ten-years time, with 49% thinking they would stay the same, and 46% thinking they would improve their position.

One might suppose that the more satisfied people were in the present, the less satisfied they might imagine themselves in the future. Individuals for whom things had gone really well so far couldn't hope for anything but stagnation and disappointment, whereas people for whom things had gone badly so far might reckon things could only get better. In fact, the opposite conclusion emerges (Fig. 2.3). The figure shows the median response to 'Where do you imagine yourself in ten years' time?' as a function of where the respondent saw herself in the present. People who are more satisfied than average in the present also believe they will be more satisfied than average in the future. In general, the expectation of the future is set just slightly above the experience to date. The diagonal line represents what you would expect if people thought the future would be the same as the past. Any response above the diagonal line represents optimism, the belief that things will be better in the future than they are in the present. Anything below the line would represent pessimism. As you can see, no group is pessimistic. The median of satisfaction in the future is never lower than the level of satisfaction in the present. It climbs like a moving bar above the level of satisfaction today; a 3 today creates the expectation of a 5 tomorrow; a 7 today creates the expectation of an 8 tomorrow. Only those who are extremely contented in their present life expect to stay the same; even they don't expect it to get worse.

Most people's happiness then, is like their appetite after the main course of a big meal. They think they are pretty full, but they could still find a way to squeeze in dessert. And if the happiness system is there to help us move towards things that might be good for us in life, then this makes good sense. No organism should ever be completely satisfied for anything more than a short

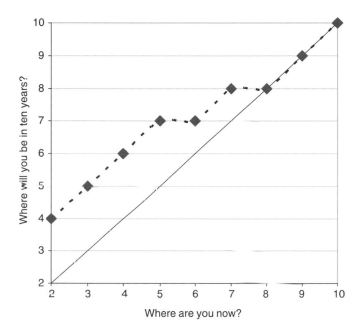

Fig. 2.3 Scale of where participants think they will be in ten years time, as a function of how they think life has turned out so far, both on a ten point scale. Data from the 2000 sweep of the National Child Development Study.

time, because there might always be some better way of doing things just around the corner, and a perfectly satisfied individual would never bother to go and discover it. Thus, whatever the circumstances, there should be a small, nagging gap between our present contentment and a conceivably possible super-contentment. Into this vital chink swarm peddlers of nostalgia, spiritual systems, drugs, and all kinds of consumer goods.

The data I have presented in this chapter, and others like them, are really a scandal. This great stage of fools on which we live is full of disappointment, conflict, pain, and death, and yet most of us go around being fairly happy. The happiness pessimists are amongst the greatest minds of modern thought. How can they have got it so wrong? How can they have failed to see that the misery of existence was so far from most people's consciousness, most of the time?

The first thing to point out is that they were all intellectuals. This means that they were probably high in the personality trait of neuroticism, about which there is more to say in Chapter 4. Angst, rumination, and isolation are part of the thinker's motivational framework and job description. Thus, the watchers of the public psyche are the group of people probably best skilled and worst qualified to do the job. Moreover, intellectuals like Schopenhauer have to cultivate a niche in the cultural field for themselves, and they won't get far by starting from the premise that things are generally OK. As any newspaper editor will tell you, that doesn't sell the product. But the idea that we might be unhappy does.

It is not just a few philosophers and poets who have been happiness pessimists. Great social and personal reform movements are almost always based on an initial premise of our unhappiness. For Marxists, the ordinary person is alienated by his non-ownership of the means of production. For Evangelists, we labour in misery until we accept His word into our hearts. And shelf after shelf in bookstores is filled with mind, body, and spirit guides whose initial axiom is that we are unfulfilled, ever more stressed, ever more empty, ever more unhappy. The uptake of all forms of therapy, dietary supplements, mood altering drugs, self-help books, relaxation treatments, and cults seems to be increasing exponentially. Whatever the relative merits of the different solutions on offer, this is an extremely interesting phenomenon. Why should a population that considers itself in general fairly happy be such desperate consumers of things supposed to cure unhappiness?

We are also very credulous when it comes to tales of

the possibility of happiness. For example, the anthropologist Margaret Mead wrote a very famous book called *Coming of age in Samoa,* in which she painted a picture of life on this Pacific island as very, well, pacific. Her Samoa is one that is free of envy, jealousy, inter-personal conflict, and violence—a happy place. As it turns out, Mead had spent not much longer in Samoa than the average round-the-world backpacker, and knew exactly what she wanted to find before she arrived. What is surprising is not Mead's (actually noble) motivation for her work of fiction, but the public response. The book became the best-selling work of anthropology of all time, and influenced the thinking of literally millions of people. Readers seemed predisposed to accept uncritically that there could be a human society with essentially no unhappiness (and to accept that Samoa was it, despite the availability of several earlier works which showed it to be a place of as much conflict and violence as anywhere else).

The premise, however, is completely ludicrous. Here is a country with far more poverty, obstetric disease, pain, and uncertainty than our own, and where the people are just as exposed as anyone to the irreduceable conflicts of being alive—love, competition, aging, and so on—and yet we seem able to accept that they were completely happy. I believe that this says more about the psychology of Mead's readers than it does about the Samoans. So we have two questions: why do we give head-space to philosophies premised on our unhappiness, when the evidence shows that in the main we are pretty happy; and why are we prone to believe that other times, places, or modes of living would be happier than our own?

For the first question, remember that judgements about happiness are fickle and sensitive to context. We may think in general that we are happy, but it would suffice to point out a few bad things about recent life, and suddenly the question looks a little different. Recall that showing photographs of attractive strangers, or drawing attention to a bad memory, is sufficient to make people reframe their own happiness judgements. Most Utopian philosophies start by pointing out something that really is vexatious in the current context. Actually, I do resent that I work all day and someone else owns the factory. Yes, I do sometimes feel lonely and purposeless. Now you point it out, I see you are right that modern living can be stressful. And reading Schopenhauer, I do see that life is in general terms, disappointing. Before you know it these isolated factors have become the frame of reference for a whole prognosis. But until they are pointed out, they don't usually seem salient enough to be the frame for our judgements.

If the happiness system exists to help us seek out the things that are best for us, then it is right that it should come very finely tuned to the possibility that things are better elsewhere. It should be constantly scanning the horizon on the lookout for a better environment, a better social network, a better mode of behaviour. And it should always have left a little space of discontent open, just in case something hoves into view which is really special. Pessimistic philosophies can exploit this little space, by drawing attention to the aspects of life that are most annoying and working them up into the whole context for decision-making. Of course, it doesn't mean that they are wrong in their diagnosis or their remedy. But it is useful to retain a balanced perspective and a critical mind.

The happiness system has not only to identify better-looking alternatives. It has to make us pursue them. Thus it is in its nature to identify things that look like they are associated with status, ease, sex, beauty, and other trappings of biological fitness, and tell us that *if we only had those circumstances*, we would be much happier. Now there may be things that make people genuinely happier, but there are also a great many things that people do that don't make them any happier at all in the long run. People *want* them, but once they have them, they become preoccupied with wanting something else. The strength of this wanting means that we are quite ready to believe that happiness *would be complete* if only some set of conditions or other were fulfilled.

In fact, though, people will never be completely happy, whatever their external conditions. The people you love won't always love you back. You yourself will be divided between irreconcilable goals, like sex and companionship, ambition and comfort, money and time. Nothing will take these conflicts away. They just have to be managed. On the other hand, the human animal is supremely capable of finding pleasures under all but the most catastrophic of circumstances. People who live on the slopes of volcanoes grow grapevines, and people with tragic personal histories find ways of being reasonably happy.

This doesn't mean that it doesn't matter what we do. There are public policies that will genuinely improve or worsen people's lives. There are also psychological strategies for narrowing the happiness gap, which will be discussed in a later chapter. However, the data presented in this chapter put frustrations into context. Things are seldom as bad as they seem. It is not the human condition to be always unhappy. If you are prone to thinking that everything in life is doom and gloom, then you might want to examine whether you are making the right comparisons, or dwelling on the past or future in the wrong way. On the other hand, this life is imperfect, and total bliss is not part of its design. Any framework that claims that any time, place, or organization of people will produce perfect happiness should be peremptorily dismissed, and Utopias should be given sceptical scrutiny. It is a disservice to people like the Samoans, who faced life with as much bravery as us, to suggest that things were one jot simpler for them than they are for us. Far from being a disappointment, this conclusion is strangely liberating. It relieves us from the anxiety that someone else's life is a paradise and ours somehow is not.

3

Love and work

Sigmund Freud is reputed to have said that the basis of well-being was 'love and work'. Freud was a happiness pessimist who had also written that the best that could be hoped for in life was 'the transformation of hysteric misery into common unhappiness'. In light of this, asking the good doctor for his prescription for good living seems a bit like, as the Nigerian proverb has it, asking a bald person for advice on your hairstyle. Nonetheless, his answer seems a reasonable one and worthy of further investigation. Which people are happier than others? Is it those with love in their lives, or fulfilling work? Is it those who earn millions, those who live a life of leisure, or those who devote themselves to a higher cause?

These are all empirical questions that psychological surveys are well capable of taking on. However, before we turn to questionnaires and correlation coefficients, it is worth considering the RIRO problem (rubbish in, rubbish out). We saw in the previous chapter that people's assessments of their own happiness are fickle and subject to all kinds of context effects and impression management. If they reflect nothing more than these, then surveys of who is happy will not mean very much.

As we have seen, almost everyone describes him or herself as moderately to very happy. Thus the amount of variation to work with is not very great. However, there is variation to explain, scattered around the upper end of the field (i.e. there are some people who are close to mid-point and others close to maximum). Though judgements of life satisfaction are affected by current mood state and other contextual factors, it seems, fortunately, that there is some genuine signal that is audible through this noise.

For one thing, when individuals are asked multiple times over a few months or years to report on their life satisfaction, the responses they give are rather (though not completely) self-consistent. When groups of people are surveyed, the results are even more consistent. Moreover, individuals' own ratings correlate with ratings of their happiness given by friends and family, and also with objective measures of things like amount of smiling, and neutral observer assessments. Besides which, the patterns reported in this chapter have been found with high consistency in multiple investigations in many countries.

Most strikingly, self-reported happiness is strongly related to health. One remarkable study examined the lives of a cohort of nuns in the USA. The nuns had written autobiographical sketches when they took holy orders. Researchers rated these for how much positive emotion they expressed. They then went on to look at the life expectancies of the sisters. This is a good natural experiment, since all nuns have diets, activity patterns, and marital and reproductive histories that are comparable to each other. It turns out that, in the quarter of the nuns who expressed most positive emotion in their sketches, 90% were still alive at age 85. In the quarter expressing least positive emotion, only 34% were still alive at that age.

This study is one of many that have found positive emotional tone to be related to better physical and mental health than unhappiness is. This is not just a correlation of two variables at a single point in time; happiness at one stage of life has also been shown to be a predictor of relative health many years later, and of responses to health shocks, like recovery times. Correlation is not causation, and none of these results proves that happiness *per se* causes a robustness in response to health challenges. However, the studies do show that people's reports of their feelings of well-being are tapping in to something that is not a mere will o' the wisp. Whatever it is they are reporting, it is on average related to something really important—robustness, stress, coping style, social support, or whatever—that in turn relates to how long they are going to live. This is just another reason for saying that people's feelings of happiness are worthy of study and promotion.

In sum, then, happiness assessments are subject to vagaries and fickleness. On the other hand, so is everything interesting that you want to measure. Psychologists are usually content to measure the ineffable on two conditions: one, that when you measure it repeatedly or using a slightly different technique, you get something close to what you got the first time (the reliability criterion); and two, that the measure you end up with is related to an objective outcome that is actually important (the validity criterion). Self-report measures of happiness generally pass these tests. Thus any patterns we might discover deserve to be taken seriously, especially where the surveys are large or the results replicated in different populations.

So who is happy? Here, once again we can turn to the NCDS survey that we first discussed in the previous chapter. Amongst the NCDS participants, as we saw, the average level of life satisfaction was 7.29 on a ten-point scale. The women in the cohort reported an average of 7.34, whereas the men's average was 7.23. This is not a large difference, but it is statistically reliable. British women of this generation are a little happier with their lot than their male peers. Is this the evidence for the crisis of the masculine role so often espoused in newspapers and magazines?

It may not be so straightforward. Many studies have found that women experience more fear and anxiety, more sadness, and particularly more of the social emotions of shame and guilt than men. Support for this is found in the NCDS in a separate part of the study where the participants were given a *malaise inventory*. This is a series of questions about negative feelings in life— misery, worry, irritability, worthlessness, and so on. Women scored significantly more highly than men; besides which, in the NCDS as in many other health studies, there was a higher instance of treatment for clinical depression among the women than among the men.

So how can women be both more miserable and happier? You will recall that the experience of negative emotions in life is largely independent of the experience of positive ones, and things like life satisfaction are affected by them both. Thus it may be that women experience more positive states than men, as well as more negative ones. There are several studies that indicate that this does indeed happen. The debate about whether the extra vividness of emotion for women is in the actual experience, or in the expression (and indeed whether, in the case of emotion, these two can entirely be teased apart) goes on. What is clear is that women in some sense do experience emotion to a slightly greater intensity than men do.

Those who say that money doesn't buy happiness don't know where to shop, or so the saying goes. So is there evidence in the NCDS that happiness comes with affluence? One measure of socio-economic position is social class. In Britain, this has usually been assessed by ranking occupations into a five-category scheme that reflects their social standing, from Class I (professional) to Class V (unskilled and routine). Life satisfaction differs across the classes, undramatically but with high statistical reliability. The highest occupational groups average about half a point higher on the ten-point scale than those in unskilled jobs (Fig. 3.1). Note that the unemployed are not included in this scheme. Other studies have shown them to have among the lowest satisfaction scores of any social group.

What is it about being in the higher social classes that increases life satisfaction? The obvious answer would be

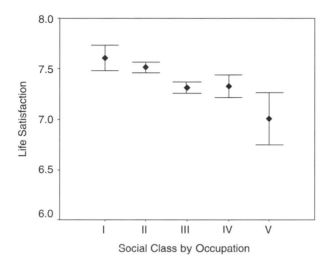

Fig. 3.1 Life satisfaction in contemporary Britain by social class, as defined by occupation. The classification runs from I, Professional to V, Unskilled and routine. Data from the 2000 sweep of the National Child Development Study.

that money brings pleasures with it. The higher social classes do have more money, and thus, in the NCDS, there is a modest correlation between income and life satisfaction. However, the social class scale reflects more than just income. It is also a measure of level of education, the likelihood of being able to choose one's work, status relationships in the workplace, and participation in non-work leisure activities. If you control statistically for income differences, there is still a relationship between life satisfaction and social class. If you control for social class, there is almost no relationship between income and life satisfaction. This suggests that it is the non-income benefits of being in a higher social class that bring increased satisfaction.

The relationship, or rather non-relationship, between income and life satisfaction is one potential explanation for a striking but consistent finding. Over the last fifty years, per capita incomes in developed countries have increased several-fold, and the increase in average happiness within these countries has been absolutely zero. For example, between 1970 and 1990, average incomes in the USA rose by 300% in real terms. There was no corresponding increase in average well-being. There is, then, a paradox. Many studies have shown a weak but consistent relationship between income and happiness at any given moment, but as everyone's income increases over time, happiness does not follow suit.

There are two possible reasons for this. One is, as mentioned earlier, that the felicitous thing about being in the higher social classes is not to do with income at all, but with some other factor. Although everyone's income has increased strikingly, the gains have been mere increases in material purchasing power, and have not actually transformed people's experience of security, meaningful goals, freedom, and so on. Although a janitor today is richer in real terms than a doctor of thirty years ago, he is still a janitor, and still has as little choice about where, when, and what he does as he ever did. The other, related possibility, is that in judgements of satisfaction, what matters above all is what one has relative to what everyone else has got.

There is evidence suggesting that both of these effects are real. Numerous studies have shown strong effects of relative rather than absolute wealth on satisfaction. As for autonomy, in the NCDS, the respondents were asked various questions about their feeling of control of their lives. Fewer than 10% of the Class Is felt that the statement 'I never really seem to get what I want' better reflected their experience than the statement 'I usually get what I want out of life'. Among the Class Vs, the proportion was 34%. Ninety-six per cent of

Class Is felt they had control over their lives, compared to only 81% of the Class Vs. Of course, 81% is still a majority, but then, as we have seen, most people think they are pretty happy and are not about to own up to being out of control of their destinies.

The answers to questions about control over life can be added up to give a 'personal control' score. This score is highest in Class I and lowest in Class V, but there is a lot of variation between individuals within a class. Personal control is a much better predictor of happiness than income is (in statistical terms, it accounts for twenty times more of the variation). The importance of personal control becomes particularly clear when individuals who are in the bottom quartile of the national income distribution but nonetheless have a high personal control score are compared to those who are in the highest quartile of income but have a low personal control score. The poor but in control group score 7.85 out of ten for life satisfaction, whereas the rich but out of control group score 5.82. Thus it seems that being at the top of the social heap only makes you happy in as much as it gives you the opportunity to control your life. If you can find alternative ways of being in control of your life, then you can be just as happy even if your income is low.

The feeling of autonomy, of being able to choose

what happens next in life, is also related to health. A series of fascinating studies of British civil servants has shown that physical health and life expectancy are linked to the grade within the service that the person works at. None of the grades suffers from absolute poverty. However, as well as higher status, the higher grades have much more control over what they do in their jobs, and this explains a significant portion of their superior outcomes. People really don't like being told what to do, whatever the material inducements.

When people get a pay rise, they are happy, even joyful. And yet we have seen that in the long term, as incomes rise, no one gets any happier. This means that there must be *adaptation*. That is to say, the initial euphoria must wear off as the person gets used to the new state, with the result that after some time, they return to the same level of happiness they had in the first place. The idea of adaptation was brought to the fore by Philip Brickman and Donald T. Campbell in a classic article in 1971. Later studies found that people who win large amounts of money in lotteries have only a temporary boost to their happiness. They return to their *ante-ludem* level of felicity in a few months, a finding that would no doubt have delighted Juvenal and the Stoics, keen as they were on pointing out the foolishness of human desires.

Brickman and Campbell created the vivid metaphor of the *hedonic treadmill* to explain the implacability of levels of happiness. Each time we advance towards a desired state, we quickly get used to the new terrain, and thus have no more satisfaction there than we did in the previous location. As a result, we work hard at running but never get anywhere. Los Angeles economist Richard Easterlin gives one of the clearest demonstrations of the hedonic treadmill at work. Participants in an ongoing social survey of a cross-section of the American population were asked to go down a list of the major consumer goods that people invest their money in (house, car, television set, travel abroad, swimming pool, second home, and so on). The first time, they were asked to tick off which of those goods formed part of their ideal of the good life (the life they would like to have). They were then asked to go down the list again and tick off which of the items they actually had already. The survey was repeated sixteen years later. Over the early part of their adult lives, people go from having few if any of these big-ticket items to having several of them. The trouble is that their ideal of what would be needed for the good life recedes at almost exactly the same rate as they advance. When they are young, a house, car, and

TV seem enough. Later on, a holiday home comes to seem just essential. Over the 16 years, people went from having 1.7 to having 3.1 items, and meanwhile the good life went from consisting of 4.4 items to consisting of 5.6 items. They were still 2 items short of where they wanted to be, just as they had been at the beginning.

This inflation goes on through the life-course, though both the attainment of new goods and the gannet-like advance of aspiration mellow in older years. As a result, in lifestyle goods, essentially no advance is achieved by accumulation, at least on average.

How do differences in life satisfaction levels between nations fit into this picture? Recall that the differences across nations are not huge. All countries basically fall in the 5 to 8 window on a ten-point scale. However, there are differences, and the Gross National Product, or wealth level, of the country, is a good predictor of these. This relationship must be squared with the apparently contradictory finding that looking within the developed countries through time, as national income has gone up, national happiness has stayed the same. It may be that increasing wealth only matters to a certain point. Some cross-sectional studies have found that the curve of national well-being against national income rises steeply when countries are poor, but levels

off once countries have reached a modest level of affluence. A related possibility, again, is that income is not
in itself productive of happiness.

Looking across the world, national income tends to
be positively related to other more nebulous variables
such as political freedom, human rights, equality, low
crime rates, and so on. These may be the things that
actually matter. Some of them, like democracy and
human rights, are achieved at a certain level of economic development and then are essentially static
against further income growth. For others, like crime or
social insecurity, economic growth initially makes great
inroads into them, but later, as all the avoidable evils
have been avoided and only the unavoidable ones
remain, further growth has ever-diminishing effects. All
this would mean that the curve of national well-being
against Gross National Product would flatten off at a
certain point, a point which the developed economies
have largely reached.

One of the most reliable findings in studies of well-
being is that people who are married score more highly
than those who are not. The NCDS is no exception. As
Fig. 3.2 shows, those who were married were consider-
ably happier than those who were not. Those cohabit-
ing were a little less happy than the married ones, with

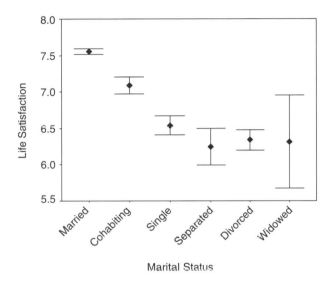

Fig. 3.2 Life satisfaction in contemporary Britain by marital status at age 42. Data fram the 2000 sweep of the National Child Development Study.

those who had never married coming in third. Least happy of all, on average, were those who had been married but were divorced, separated, or widowed.

The information on which the figure is based was collected in 2000, when the NCDS cohort was 42 years of age. Most of the participants were married by this time, and theirs was a generation where marriage was the norm. The patterns might not hold so strongly in a group where marriage is not so widespread and culturally expected. Nonetheless, these are relatively strong effects. Marital status accounts for much more of the variation in life satisfaction than social class does. Moreover, essentially the same pattern is found in numerous independent studies.

There has been much interest in the idea that men and women might benefit to differing extents from marriage. Studies of life satisfaction give only slight support to this idea. In the NCDS, the excess happiness of married women over never-married ones was 1.05 points, whereas the comparable gap for men was 0.97 points. The divorced-married gap was 1.28 for women compared to 1.16 for men. The sex differences are modest, especially when you allow for women's greater emotional expressivity in general. All in all, it looks like marriage, or the lack of it, has similar effects for women and for men.

Before we jump to the conclusion that Dr. Freud was right about love, and good biblical love at that, being the key to happiness, we ought to consider the patterns a little more deeply. It has often been claimed that these findings show that marriage is the most enduring path to happiness. However, it could equally well be that happiness is the most enduring path to marriage. Extroverts tend to fall into romantic relationships more easily than introverts, and they tend to be happier, too. On the other hand, those who are constitutionally neurotic tend to be unhappy, and they are at a heightened risk of divorce. Thus, part of the effect is due to people who are happier at the outset getting married more, and staying married longer, rather than matrimony bringing joy.

There seems to be consensus that this cannot be the whole explanation, but the only way to know for sure is to follow the same individuals through time as they go from single days to matrimony (or not). This was the strategy taken by a German study that recontacted the same panel of 24,000 people yearly for up to 15 years. The study showed that, indeed, those who got married were happier at the outset than those who did not. However, this is not the whole story. The transition to marriage in an individual was also associated with a substantial increase in happiness over and above whatever baseline they were at. Within two years, though, this hike had generally melted away, and they were essentially back at baseline. Interestingly, the researchers observed considerable variation in the response to marriage. People who responded with a very large increase in happiness in the short term retained that increment for many years. On the other hand, some people, whose initial reaction to marriage was relatively weak, were actually less happy a couple of years later than at the outset. And the study only included those who stayed in their marriages.

The same researchers also looked at widowhood, and here they found greater evidence of lasting effects. Perhaps some things are never quite got used to. If so, this would be a case of an endowment effect; that is, losing something you have is worse than not having had it in the first place.

There is thus some uncertainty about why the marriage effects are so strong, and other studies suggest that adaptation is not so quick and complete as the German data appear to show. My preferred explanation for the NCDS pattern is that marital transitions (in either direction) cause quite a large short-term deviation in happiness. Given that the NCDS cohort were 42 years old at the time of asking, quite a few of the married ones would have been literally in their honeymoon period, whereas quite a few of the divorced ones would have been in the throes or immediate aftermath of their divorces. These individuals, who were still feeling the short-term effects of their marital transition, will have affected the averages for their respective groups quite significantly. It doesn't mean that individuals don't adapt, given a little more time. Thus, the relative strength of effect of marital status compared to, say, social class, might be a function of the fact that more people were in the midst of changing marital status than they were of changing social class, rather than anything else.

Is there anything to which we definitely do not adapt? The best candidates turn out to be a revealing assortment. Although people with acquired disabilities or health problems show very considerable adaptation, the adaptation is often not quite complete, leaving a shadow in their happiness judgements. In the NCDS, those who have any kind of long-standing illness or disability that impairs their work have a mean life satisfaction of 6.49, compared to 7.39 for those who do not. This is nearly as great a gap as the single-married one.

Another domain where complete adaptation is elusive is exposure to noise. For example, residents were interviewed four months after a new road opened in their neighbourhood. They were irritated by the noise, but most felt that they would eventually adapt. One year on, they were just as irritated, and had become more pessimistic about the possibility of ever adaptating. There is little evidence that people ever do. This is an interesting case because, in general, people underestimate their own capacity to adapt to a negative life event. In this case, they thought they could adapt and in fact could not.

Finally, one might think that the availability of cosmetic breast surgery could lead to a kind of mam-mamorphic treadmill, with women who have had alter-ations immediately as dissatisfied with their bodies as they had been before. Much as one might like to believe this to be the case, there is some evidence that the improvement in well-being is real and lasting. Several studies report increased body and life satisfaction, and decreased psychiatric problems, amongst women who have had breast procedures.

Our implicit theory of happiness says that it is strongly related to our life circumstances. We would not strive to get pay rises, new cars, and people to go to bed with us, if we felt that we were just pouring sand into a bottomless container that foolish humanity has been failing to fill since time immemorial. But the conclusion that at least some psychologists have drawn from the data on life circumstances and happiness is that nothing makes much difference. It seems as if there is a set level of happiness to which we will return more or less whatever we do.

Though this idea contains a great deal of truth, the situation is probably more interesting and more complex. We can adapt differentially to different aspects of life. Basic threats to the safety of the individual— chronic cold, food shortage, or excessive environmental noise, are things that you would never get used to. Serious health problems can leave a lasting mark. The lack of autonomy in life is an enduring negative, leading ultimately not just to unhappiness but to poor health. On the other hand, income and material goods are quickly and completely adapted to, and so as economic growth ploughs on, people will not necessarily get any happier, depending on how that growth is used in terms of quality of life. Aptly intermediate between noise and money is marriage. This produces a large deviation in the short to medium term, but significant adaptation in the end.

The economist Robert Frank has distinguished between positional and non-positional goods. For non-positional goods, the happiness we derive from them is not predicated on a comparison with what anyone else has. Health and freedom are non-positional goods in this sense. Positional goods have a different psychology. We are satisfied with our income or the size of our car in comparison with the incomes and cars we see around us. Frank argues that this positional psychology is an adaptive evolutionary legacy. We have evolved in environments where there were numerous possible ways of making one's living, and our reproductive success would have been dependent not on absolute health but on relative status. Since it was impossible to know inherently what the optimal behaviour in local conditions would be, we evolved a psychology of looking at those around us who seemed to be doing best, and trying to do even better than them. This leads to competition very much like that observed between trees in tropical forests. Trees have no inherent theory about how tall it is good to be. They merely need to be taller than those around them in order to get some light. As a result of vying for light, forests get taller and taller until vast amounts of time and lignin have been expended in pushing the canopy—pointlessly—hundreds of feet into the air. If all trees were one tenth of their height, no individual tree would be worse off, and all those exhausting sapling years could be avoided. But since light access is positional, it can't happen.

Frank implies that marriage is non-positional, and so, faced with a choice of investing time earning or investing it in your relationship, the latter will bring more lasting fulfilment in the long term. Wholesome as this view might be, it may be an overstatement. Even marriage shows evidence of adaptation, and moreover, in societies that are polygynous or serially monogamous like ours, men seek nubile new wives as status goods. However, Frank's insight is absolutely correct in the following respect. Our implicit theory of happiness will always try to fool us into thinking that amassing more positional goods—keeping up with the Joneses—will make us happier in the long run, but, objectively, this will not happen. On the other hand, health, autonomy, social embededness, and the quality of the environment are real sources of happiness.

This conclusion really matters. We can easily be dismissive of the colleague who says he is going to give up the rat race and build boats in his shed for a poor but independent livelihood. But he probably *will* be happier, due to differential adaptation to autonomy and income. He just needs to overcome the siren urgings of positional psychology. There are public policy implications, too. As I write, the British Government is planning a major expansion of airports all over the country. However, hedonics predicts that people will soon adapt to the availability of cheap regional flights in Europe, and find them just as tiresome as the longer train journeys they replace. On the other hand, we will never adapt to the increased noise.

We can then, in principle, be rational and evidence-based about how we set up our lives. This raises an immediate problem. Social scientists have generally assumed that people *know* what makes them happy. Indeed, this assumption is deeply embedded in economic theory, which says that people's choices between competing goods are driven by their maximization of the *utility* they get. When people decide to consume A rather than B, this means that they get more utility from A. If they got more utility from B, they would choose B instead. Thus, if people really would get more utility taking less income and having greater leisure and autonomy, then they would have done so, and wouldn't need psychologists to tell them.

As we have seen, this turns on how we interpret the meaning of utility. If the utility of A relative to B is taken to mean the relative propensity to choose A over B, then it is necessarily true that people will always maximize their utility. The evidence that they choose maximal utility is that they prefer A over B, and the evidence that A has greater utility than B is the fact that they choose it. However, this says nothing about individual or aggregate happiness before, during, or after the process of choosing. On the other hand, if utility is taken to mean something psychologically real like happiness, then we seem to be left with the extraordinary conclusion that everyone is as happy as they could possibly be, all the time, since if there were something they could do which would yield greater happiness, they would have done it. Everything is for the best since we live in the best of all possible worlds.

This conclusion is not justified, since it is clear that people do not always make choices that maximize their happiness. For one thing, the well-being I might receive from choosing something depends on what everyone else chooses. I might be content with a tiny car or even a bicycle, as long as everyone else drives one too, freeing up thousands of pounds for something else. But if the roads are full of Landcruisers with enormous bull-bars, then my moped is going for a trade-in. In a world of high crime, I need to choose to invest in burglar alarms and housing outside of the town centre, but this does not mean that I am thereby happier than in a world where I live ten minutes from work.

Even more importantly, our choices in life are driven not by our actual experience of happiness, but by our implicit theory of happiness. This theory tends to say that positional goods and status are important, that the rat race is worth running, that a beautiful wife will change my life, and so on. This theory is not derived from experience and departs significantly from reality. Thus we are always prone to being tricked by it into making choices that do not maximize happiness. Why we should have this stubborn implicit theory is a subject we return to in a later chapter.

Worriers and enthusiasts

Common experience shows that some people are cheerful and buoyant almost whatever bad things happen to them, whilst some are full of worry and anguish even in the best of circumstances. In fact, it is very easy to find, amongst people you know, two individuals roughly matched for age, income, occupation, and marital status, of whom one is always positive and upbeat, and the other prone to suspicion, disappointment, and anxiety. We saw in the previous chapter that changes in objective life circumstances lead to only modest changes in happiness, and even these are subject to adaptation. So what explains the deeper, more enduring happiness differences between people?

Such differences do exist, and are real. Self-reports of happiness and well-being are fairly stable, even over periods of several years. For example, one large study examined reports of happiness and well-being in the same individuals 7 to 12 years apart, and found a very substantial correlation between the scores at the two time periods. Life events will make only a modest difference to this picture. Studies have contrasted people with stable life circumstances and those going through major life upheavals, or those with rising incomes and those with falling incomes, and they still find that the best predictor of how happy people are at the end of the study is how happy they were at the beginning. It is as if happiness or unhappiness stem in large part from how we address what happens in the world, not what actually happens.

Further evidence for this view comes from the fact that people who are happy in their jobs are also happy in their hobbies. If happiness depended mainly upon the objective situation, then you might think that people who found their jobs horrible would develop their hobbies and be especially happy in them, whilst people who loved their jobs would itch for Monday morning to get back into action. In fact, the more enjoyment people get from Monday to Friday, the more they get evenings and weekends too. Some people just get more enjoyment.

Perhaps most strikingly, identical twins are more similar in their happiness than ordinary siblings or fraternal twins. David Lykken and Auke Tellegen asked pairs of identical twins for reports on their happiness on two occasions nine years apart. They found that the happiness of twin A in the first year predicted the happiness of twin A nine years later, and also that the happiness of twin A in year one was correlated with the happiness of twin B in year one. Most strikingly, though, they found that if you wanted to predict twin B's happiness in year nine, you could use twin A or twin B's happiness in year one more or less interchangeably and get the same result. In pairs of identical twins who had been separated at birth and raised apart, the correlation in happiness was just as high as in those who had been brought up together. Given that identical twins are genetic clones of one another, this is powerful evidence that some inherited factors guide our lives powerfully towards a certain level of perceived well-being, almost regardless of the environment we live in.

So what is the nature of the inherent psychological differences that make some people characteristically happier than others? Psychologists refer to stable between-individual differences in classes of behaviour using the same concept used in ordinary language—personality. A personality characteristic is some attribute of a person that is stable across time (if someone was very nervous one day but not at all the next, then you could not really say that nervousness was part of their personality). It must also be stable across situations. If a person is nervous only in cars but in no other contexts, then that looks like an idiosyncrasy, perhaps learned from a car accident, rather than a personality trait. Finally, there has to be variation between individuals for something to count as a personality trait. The presence of anxious thoughts after having been put into a pool full of hungry sharks would not be a good candidate for a personality measure, as pretty much everyone would be about as anxious as it is possible to be in such a context. Anxious thoughts whilst walking through a strange city would be a much better discriminator, since some people would have a lot whilst others would have none at all.

Several different typologies of personality dimensions have been put forward, and it is beyond the scope of this book to weigh them up. What is noteworthy, though, is that pretty much all of them agree on two fundamental dimensions, both of which are relevant to happiness. The first dimension is to do with the experience of negative emotions. Every human being, indeed every mammal and perhaps every vertebrate, has systems for detecting negative events in their environment (negative in terms of their potential impact on the individual's biological fitness). For example, the kind of negative events that are out there in the typical human environment are rejection by important others, ostracism from the group, predation, disease, lack of resources, attack by strangers, and so on. These negative possibilities have their particular suite of associated emotions: fear, worry, shame, guilt, and so on. There are also physical and cognitive changes associated with them. The physical changes include increases in heart rate and diversion of blood from the guts to the musculature. The cognitive changes include increased vigiliance, especially to potentially threatening stimuli, dwelling on potentially negative information, and mental rumination on possible outcomes.

These vital systems are present in us all, but their tuning seems to vary somewhat from individual to individual. Absolutely all personality studies find that a major and reliable discriminator between people is the degree to which they are affected by worry, fear, and other negative emotions. The dimension that measures this variation is called neuroticism or negative emotionality. A person's place along this dimension is not only stable over time but appears to be set at least partly by heredity. Neuroticism scores are produced from people's responses to questions like 'Do you worry a lot?' and 'Do you sometimes feel blue for no reason?' Such questions might seem a bit simplistic and prone to all kinds of response biases, but in fact neuroticism scores are rather stable and are very good predictors of real outcomes like long-term health, relationship behaviour, and proneness to depression and anxiety. Thus the scores mean something. This is the mystery of personality psychology; questionnaires that look flaky actually turn out to work surprisingly well. People must really know themselves, and particularly where they stand relative to others in the population, or the scores would not be such good predictors as they are.

The second major dimension of personality that most systems agree on is to do with positive emotions, or at least, positive motivations. This dimension is captured by such labels as extroversion, behavioural approach, and sensation seeking. High scorers provide affirmative answers to questions like 'I am the life of the party'. In ordinary language, extroversion is equated with sociability. Whilst it is true that extroverts tend to have more friends, be more talkative, and go out more, there is also a non-social side to the trait. Extroverts enjoy travel and change in their routines, prefer dangerous sports or exuberant hobbies, like more sex partners and sexual experimentation, have more of a sweet tooth, and are in danger of drinking too much or getting addicted to drugs. They are quicker to get married (perhaps because they are good at meeting people), but also more likely to be unfaithful (ditto) than their more introverted peers.

The best contemporary explanation of extroversion is as follows. There is a schedule of things that can occur in the environment that, over evolutionary time, have consistently increased our ancestors' biological fitness when they have pursued them. The most obvious examples are things that are sweet like ripe fruits, the pursuit of game or new habitats, sex with attractive people, and, since we are a deeply social species depending on group living for all aspects of our survival, the company of others in general. Evolution needed to provide a way of ensuring that opportunities for these kinds of thing got taken whenever they cropped up, so they have all been tagged with a kind of immediate rewarding-ness that makes us want them. This incentive value can wreak havoc with our best laid plans. Should I study or go round to a friend's party? Should I stop now or have a sweet dessert? Should I invest this money or spend it on skiing, diving, or mountaineering? Should I buy the magazine with the better editorial coverage or the one with the strikingly healthy young woman on the cover? Huge swathes of our cultural and economic life, from the multi-billion pound confectionery industry to the even larger sex industry, are based on the fact that certain products, by pressing the right incentive buttons, have a fast track to human decision-making centres.

These incentives are rewarding to all of us, but the strength of the pull varies somewhat between individuals, and in extroverts it is stronger than in introverts. I think of the difference between the extrovert and the introvert in the following way. Imagine walking through a crowded bazaar. Each stall offers a different and delightful ware, from the wholesome to the adventurous through the morally dubious to the illegal, including things you imbibe, experiences you can have, and welcoming-looking gatherings of other people. Everything is enjoyable. You can choose to walk on by, perhaps to carry out some important task for which you are crossing the bazaar, or you can pause and take some delight or other. Every stall has a stall-holder, promoting his particular merchandise. For the introvert, the stall-holders are subdued and not always convincing. For the extrovert, the stall holders are loud and charismatic, capturing attention, and before you know it . . . .

The psychological mechanisms controlling, for example, sexual behaviour and food appetite, are probably quite separate. However, all of the positively rewarding behaviours seem to draw on a common mechanism of incentive pull. It is this common mechanism that is tuned differently in introverts and extroverts. This explains why extroverts tend to behave differently from introverts not just in any one domain, but across several. For example, they are more sociable *and* enjoy more active sports, or are more libidinous *and* have a sweet tooth.

It is time to relate these two major personality dimensions to happiness. For neuroticism, the prediction is obvious. Neuroticism is the tendency to experience unpleasant feelings like worry and fear, feelings which, at least on a momentary basis, are inconsistent with happiness. Therefore, the higher people score on the neuroticism dimension, the less happy they should be.

We recently gave a personality inventory to nearly 600 members of the British public through our online psychology laboratory. We also asked them how happy they were overall, on a scale of 1 to 5. The sample was very broad in terms of age and social class. Neuroticism scores were strong predictors of self-reported happiness (Fig. 4.1). As you can see, those scoring in the lowest quartile for neuroticism are free of care, and scoring around 4 on the 5-point scale of happiness. The top quartile of neuroticism scorers are barely above the mid-point. About 17% of the variance in happiness was accounted for by neuroticism, making it one of the strongest predictors known.

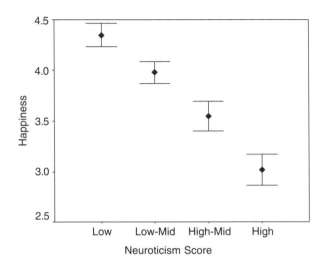

Fig. 4.1 Average happiness rating of British adults on a 5 point scale by neuroticism personality score. The four groups are formed by creating quartiles from the distribution of scores. N = 574.

The correlation between neuroticism and unhappiness has often been found in the corresponding literature before, and is perhaps not too astonishing, given that part of the definition of neuroticism involves negative emotion, and that neuroticism scales can contain questions like, 'Do you often feel miserable?' More sophisticated studies have separated happiness out into two sub-components, both of which contribute to the overall judgement of happiness. The first is negative happiness: 'How often do you feel really unhappy?' whilst the second is positive happiness: 'How often do you feel really happy?' These two are fairly independent of each other, since the answer to both could be 'often'. As you might predict, neuroticism is a good predictor of the negative happiness rating, but not of the positive rating. At least high neuroticism scorers can have plenty of joy in between all that worry.

These findings look like bad news for neurotics. They are prone to dissatisfaction and unhappiness. However, it is consoling to recall that level two happiness is not the only human good. Many studies have shown that creative and influential individuals in the arts and public life are higher than average in neuroticism. In some important sense, it is their dissatisfaction that drives them to achieve in domains humanity counts as valuable, so as long as outright psychiatric illness can be avoided, it is better to see neuroticism as a mixed blessing, with certain signature strengths, rather than a handicap.

The prediction for the relationship between extroversion and happiness is a little less straightforward. As we have seen, extroverts want rewarding things more strongly than introverts do. However, it doesn't follow that they should be any happier. It could even be the other way around. With so many things that they crave, they might be dissatisfied much of the time. Moreover, wanting things strongly is not the same as liking them once you have them, as we shall see in a later chapter.

In fact, extroverts do tend to be happier. The relationship between extroversion and happiness score in our online study is shown in Fig. 4.2. Other studies have also shown this pattern, and demonstrated the mirror-image pattern to neuroticism. That is to say, extroverts have more positive emotion, but can have just as much negative emotion as anyone else. If it is any consolation, the cheery socialite can have moments of existential dread and pain just like anyone else.

I think the most likely explanation for the greater happiness of extroverts is that they are more likely to do things with a strong emotional reward. At any given point in time, your extrovert is more likely to be married, more likely to have been to a party, more likely to

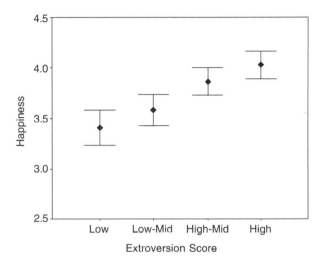

Fig. 4.2 Average happiness rating of British adults on a 5 point scale by extroversion score. The four groups are formed by creating quartiles from the set of scores. N = 567.

have been playing sports, more likely to have talked to friends, and has had sex more recently, than your introvert. His personality leads him to draw a series of moments of reward from the environment. Thus when you ask him, he is differentially likely to be in a positive affective state. People who rate their happiness as unusually high are low-neuroticism extroverts who spend little time alone. Thus, at the moment of asking, they are more likely to have just come from some social interaction or other.

Once again, it might seem that greater extroversion is an unalloyed benefit, since extroverts report themselves to be happier. However, in recent studies we have found that the restlessness of extroverts makes their family lives unstable in the long term. Moreover, they have an increased risk of serious accidents and hospitalizations. Nothing in life is without a downside, and thus the slightly greater happiness of extroverts is not necessarily to be envied, but merely seen as a trade-off.

There are other personality dimensions that correlate with happiness. Individuals who score highly on scales of agreeableness and conscientiousness also tend to be happier. The determination of happiness by personality, then, seems to happen in two ways. First, there are direct influences. Some personality traits control the tuning of emotion systems; that is, how easily emotion systems go off. This obviously has a direct effect on happiness. Then there are indirect effects; personality traits which determine the way we schedule and rank the possible behaviours in our environment. In the case of extroversion, high scorers spend more time in social interaction and other pleasurable activities. In the case of conscientiousness and agree-ableness, high scorers may get things done, yielding a feeling of satisfaction, or be nice to others, yielding reciprocal and felicific favours in turn. The distinction between direct and indirect effects is important for the question of which aspects of happiness can be deliberately manipulated, and how.

The discovery of these stable temperamental determin-ants of happiness has been an extremely important one (though, let us face it, it is something we all suspected). It seemed to make sense of the findings that the associ-ations between happiness and things like wealth and marital situation are rather weak. Indeed, it even sug-gests that such associations as there are between life circumstances and happiness may not be what they seem. For example, in our online data, married people are happier than single people, as we would expect. However, they are also less neurotic, and this is likely to be a cause rather than a consequence of their marital status. We know that neurotic people's relationships are disproportionately likely to break up, so many of them probably won't make it into matrimony.

When you control statistically for the differences in neuroticism, the happiness gap between the single and the married is only about half what it is in the uncorrected data. Thus the causal effect of marriage may not be as strong as we would have supposed (and even this is probably subject to adaptation in the long term, as we saw in the last chapter). What seems like an effect of life circumstances on happiness is really, at least in part, an effect of personality on life circumstances.

This could be quite a general phenomenon. In a famous study, Bruce Headey and Alexander Wearing of the University of Melbourne set out to examine the relative contributions of personality and life events to happiness by repeatedly interviewing a panel of several residents of Victoria over a number of years. The direction of their investigation was soon coloured by their observation that the same kinds of events kept happening to the same people. Thus, in the end, rather than treating life events and personality as two independent sources of influence on happiness, they looked at how personality influences life events.

It turns out that high neuroticism scorers simply have more bad things happen to them. Their financial affairs and their social relationships are unsettlingly likely to go belly-up. Extroverts, on the other hand, are more likely to experience changes for the better in many life domains. Individuals high in another dimension, called Openness to Experience, just had more things happen to them, both good and bad. This dimension is not correlated with happiness, possibly because the good things and the bad things cancel each other out.

We know that in this study, causality cannot run from life events to personality scores, since the study assessed personality in the first interview, and life events in subsequent years (and personality scores are very stable over time anyway). There are potential methodological confounds, though. High neuroticism scorers tend to exaggerate negative events, and are also differentially likely to remember the negative aspects of things. Thus, faced with assessing whether a life event like 'serious argument with children' or 'continuous financial worry' has happened to them over the last two years, they could be likely to conclude that it had even though their objective situation is no worse than anyone else's. However, there are some events—like getting married, getting divorced, or getting sacked—that leave little room for ambiguity or selective memory. They either happened this year or they did not. In the Headey and Wearing study, and in others, the occurrence of these objective events is related to neuroticism and extroversion and rather consistent over time. Some people just keep having catastrophes, and others always land buttered-side up.

How can this be the case, given that events like these seem to come from sources external to the person? Neuroticism is a predictor of vulnerability to depression, as well as many forms of physical ill health, so the life events involving health will obviously be related to it. Health has knock-on consequences in the career domain (unfortunately, it is hard to get promoted if you miss a lot of work due to illness), and probably in family life too. Depression, in particular, can be very damaging in social and marital relationships, and it leads to poor decisions of all kinds. High neuroticism scorers will often end up reaping the consequences of decisions made when depressed.

For extroversion, it is harder to see the link. Extroverts will tend to take more risks, but one would imagine that would increase negative outcomes as well as positive ones. Their enthusiasm and positive energy may often prove self-fulfilling prophecies, and their greater sociability could certainly mean that they attract networks of people keen to contribute to the enterprise, who may then be there to catch them if they fall.

The Australian study shows that part of the association between happiness and life events is really an indirect association between personality and happiness. This means that when we examine the relationship between life circumstances and happiness, as we did in the previous chapter, we almost certainly *overestimate* how important life events are. Having said that, Headey and Wearing concluded that life events did have a genuine effect on well-being over and above the indirect operation of personality, although for each event this effect would be subject to adaptation over time.

Let us summarize the main factors associated with differences in happiness reviewed in this chapter and the last. The best way of doing this is to consider the amount of variation accounted for by each factor. This is the method statisticians use for thinking about the relative strengths of a whole list of influences on some outcome. For example, if we had to predict as accurately as possible how happy someone was, and knew absolutely nothing about him or her, then we would just guess. If we had any sense, we would do this by choosing the average score for the population. Comparing our prediction to the true score, we would make a certain amount of error. Now suppose somebody gives us one piece of information about the person in question. If that type of information accounts for 100% of the variation in happiness in the population we are study-ing, then we can now predict with absolute accuracy the target person's happiness. Our error would be zero. If on the other hand, the type of information we have been given only accounts for only 1% of the variation in happiness, then we would be only slightly better off than if we were guessing—our error would be, on average, 99% as large as it was when guessing. And if the infor-mation accounted for 50% of the variation, then our error would be half its previous size, and so on. We can thus tabulate, for various types of information, how much variation in happiness is accounted for when this information is introduced (Table 4.1).

Even this very simple analysis, which makes no attempt to tease apart the relationships the different factors have with each other, makes it quite clear that factors internal to the person have a larger effect than those that are features of his or her objective situation. If you want to know how happy Bob will be in ten years' time, don't bother to think about the fact that he will then be in his forties, or that he is a man. Don't con-sider the fact that he is a dentist who will by then be in the top 5% of wage earners and have a huge house in the country. Don't even factor into your deliber-ations the beautiful and voluptuous wife he will meet or the three children she will bear him. Instead, have him

Table 4.1 Estimates of the proportion of the inter-individual variation in happiness accounted for by various factors considered one at a time. Note that indirect pathways (for example from neuroticism via marital status to happiness) have not been modelled and thus the importance of some situational factors is if anything overestimated.

Factor	Variation accounted for
Sex	1%
Age	1%
Income	3%
Social class	4%
Marital status	6%
Neuroticism	6–28%
Extroversion	2–16%
Other personality factors	8–14%

take a personality inventory. Alternatively, for the best estimate of all, simply ask him how happy he is right now.

This is rather a sobering conclusion, and it leads some people to a gloomy prognosis. If your set point of happiness is determined by your temperament, it seems to imply that it doesn't much matter what you try to do. Your level of happiness will remain stubbornly unmoved for more than a few feeble days. As Lykken and Tellegen put it in their report of the twin research, 'It may be that trying to be happier is as futile as trying to be taller and therefore is counterproductive.' Surely this makes much legitimate human aspiration a hollow farce. People make choices because they believe that one alternative will make them happier than the other. They must believe this, or they would be indifferent, resigned, and ultimately disaffected.

There are two responses to this point of despair. First, there is a difference between 'not often changed', and 'not changeable'. Most people's running stamina declines with age, for biological reasons, but some start training in mid-life and thus deliberately counteract this trend. There is a popular perception that 'biological' factors are somehow immobile and deterministic whilst 'social' factors somehow leave hope and room for human freedom. In fact, things that have biological causes are not necessarily more or less changeable than things that have social causes. For example, let us suppose that we had discovered that happiness is entirely determined by income. In the society in which we live, it is simply impossible for most people to radically increase their income, and indeed, income at 25 years old is a pretty good predictor of income at 55 years old. Thus, people would be denied the possibility of change, though the cause was not biological. For me, the personality findings show that happiness stems mainly not from the world itself, but from the way people address the world. This is one of the few things in life you can work on directly. You have all the resources you need to do it available already, and it is probably easier to change yourself than it is to change the whole of your external circumstances (it is certainly a lot cheaper). And the life-events studies suggest that if you can change yourself, the external world may even begin to follow suit.

As we have seen, neuroticism is the strongest single predictor of unhappiness. High neuroticism scorers will always be *vulnerable* to negative thoughts and feelings. That they cannot change. However, there are techniques in which they can train themselves that seem to have quite a marked effect on how they deal with this vulnerability, which can make a great deal of difference to their being in the world. Such techniques are discussed in Chapter 6. And as for extroversion, the high scorer will not need to decide to make friends or do lots of sport, since these things will loom out of the fog and seduce him. The low scorer may need to consciously remind himself that these things are sources of pleasure. His capacity to enjoy them once he has done this can be just as strong as anyone else's. He just has to work at initiating them more deliberately.

More broadly, the conclusion that, since happiness is immutable, human action is pointless assumes that happiness in a narrow sense is the only good worth seeking. This is not so. Human choices have a point not just because of their impact on feelings of pleasure and worry but also because of their effects on broader goods like interest, equity, beauty, justice, harmony, and community. Thus the lesson of the personality studies might be that, apart from negative cognition so serious that it stops you functioning, you should not be completely preoccupied by the level of felt joy and worry. As Martin Seligman has argued, sweating over changing these things will have only limited effect. Instead, you have to learn to put them into context and lift your eyes beyond them to the broader horizon.

5

Wanting and liking

Aldous Huxley's prophetic novel *Brave new world* (1931) depicts an England where unhappiness has been eliminated. 'Everybody's happy now' is the mantra repeated to the young 150 times a night for the first twelve years of life. Perfect happiness is ensured by a combination of genetic engineering, artificially controlled growth conditions, and intense mind-training from an early age. However, for any residual glimmers of dissatisfaction that somehow survive into adulthood, there is *soma*. Soma is a synthetic drug which the population is encouraged, almost required, to use on a daily basis. It banishes all feelings of discontent; 'one cubic centimetre cures ten gloomy sentiments'. As well as getting people through their working week, soma can be used for social control. Puffing an aerosol of soma into the air easily disperses a riot that threatens to turn into a revolution.

Though Huxley's satire is astonishingly perceptive

and fresh today, most of the technical aspects of his vision—growing babies in jars, for example—are as far-fetched and implausible as they were when he wrote them. What about soma? Could there really be a drug whose specific action would be to produce a state of happiness? This implies that happiness has a specific locus in the brain that it would be possible to manipulate. Is there any evidence of what such a locus might be?

The most obvious equivalents to soma in real life are antidepressants like Prozac. Prozac (the trade name of the compound fluoxetine) was the first of a new generation of antidepressants called the selective serotonin reuptake inhibitors (SSRIs). Before the advent of the SSRIs, antidepressants had been rather effective at dealing with clinical depression, but had produced a wide range of side-effects, often including sedation, weight gain, blurred vision, and a dry mouth. The SSRIs were about equally effective at treating the depression, but with fewer of these side-effects. Indeed, at least a sub-group of patients reported feeling 'better than well' with the new drugs. In healthy volunteers with no history at all of depressive illness, taking an SSRI increases measures of extroversion and positive emotion. The effect is not dramatic, but it is detectable. SSRIs proved effective in treating a wide range of conditions, including, for example, social phobia, a disorder of extreme shyness that scarcely existed before the drug was found to cure it.

The reception of the SSRIs has been astonishing. Prozac was launched, in the USA first, in 1988. Over the following ten years, antidepressant use rose by 100–200% in many developed countries, including the UK and USA, and much of this was due to the uptake of the SSRIs. Rates of use continue to grow at 6–10% per year, with over 3% of the population taking SSRIs in the UK and USA at any one time. For sufferers from clinical depression, SSRIs are a lifeline, but there are probably many people out there who seek them simply because they want a chemical shelter from the normal pains of being human. Some evidence for this comes from the fact that rates of use in Germany and France are less than half that in economically comparable Britain.

Prozac is not soma. Its effects in healthy volunteers are subtle, and moreover, it needs a few weeks of taking the drug for the effects to kick in. This is thought to be because the action of the drug on the relevant systems is quite indirect. The SSRI disables a mechanism whose function is to remove the important brain messenger chemical serotonin; levels of serotonin at one end of certain brain cells are augmented; the cells retune and become more active; and this causes an increase in serotonin activity at the other end of the cell. Only then does the antidepressant action follow. Soma, by contrast, produced positive feelings and ended negative thoughts in minutes.

Amazingly, though, a candidate soma has recently been discovered. This compound, d-fenfluramine, directly stimulates activity in serotonin-using brain cells. In a key study, participants were given a questionnaire of negative attitudes and thoughts. The questionnaire asked them to endorse items such as 'If I do not do as well as other people, it means I am an inferior human being' as true or false. Cunningly, the participants just did one half of the questionnaire at the beginning of the experiment. Under normal circumstances, performance on the two halves is highly consistent.

The volunteers then took a pill of either d-fenfluramine or an inert substance. One hour later they took the second half of the questionnaire. The d-fenfluramine group showed a reduction in negative thoughts and beliefs, whereas the control group showed no change. 'One gram banishes ten negative thoughts!'

The cognitive effects of d-fenfluramine are a new discovery, and much remains to be worked out about how it feels, how long it lasts, and how widespread its effects are. D-fenfluramine had previously been proposed as a treatment for obesity, but concerns about cardiac side-effects led to its abandonment, and these problems will probably prevent its development as an anti-depressant.

Serotonin, the target brain chemical for d-fenfluramine and SSRIs, has entered public consciousness as 'the happiness chemical', so much so that psychology books have subtitles like 'Treating a low serotonin society'. So is serotonin really the brain locus of happiness? And if so, what does it do, why is it there and what do we know about its interactions with the rest of the brain? In fact, as it turns out, the situation is complex, with many brain systems involved in desire, pleasure and contentment. However, we are starting to understand these systems, and their organization sheds intriguing light on the way happiness works.

The PET scanner is a window on the brain. This machine consists of a ring of sensors, placed around the head, that detect radioactivity, and, by triangulation, localize its source with great precision. The subject has been injected a few minutes earlier with a form of glucose that gives off a radioactive signal. Wherever this glucose goes within the brain, it will be traceable by the radiation it gives off. Glucose flows to whichever brain cells are metabolically active, so the map of the brain produced by the scanner is effectively a map of which parts of the brain are working hard at that moment in time.

When a cocaine addict lying in the PET machine thinks about smoking crack, there are two areas inside the middle of the brain that are particularly active. These are known as the amygdala and the nucleus accumbens. The role of the amygdala in emotional reactions has long been understood. It is hyperactive in depression and anxiety, and when it is removed or damaged in both animals and people, there is an odd syndrome where the processing of emotions is impaired. Experimental monkeys and rats with no amygdalas lose their ability to discriminate emotional value, failing to fear things that should be feared, whilst eating non-foods and attempting to mate with unsuit-able targets. Conversely, stimulating the amygdala can make them excessively afraid. Humans with amygdala damage due to disease or brain surgery lose the ability to recognize the expression of fearful emotions, for example on faces or in tones of voice. The amygdala is not just involved in the negative emotions, though. When a monkey feels the sweet taste of fruit juice on its tongue, or sees the juice container coming round, there is a volley of activity in the amygdala. Thus the best interpretation of what the amygdala does is that it acts as an 'emotional hub', tagging incoming perceptual information with an appropriate emotional response.

The amygdala is close to, and intimately connected with, the nucleus accumbens. The nucleus accumbens is the receiving end of an important tract of neurons (that is, brain cells) that run forward deep inside the brain, and which communicate with each other using the chemical dopamine. When a stimulant such as morphine is diffused into the nucleus accumbens of a rat, the rat wants to feed. If, on the other hand, neurons in the dopamine tract leading to the nucleus accumbens are suppressed with different drugs, rats will not bother to pick up a reward such as tasty food that is on the other side of the cage.

The natural interpretation of what this dopamine system is doing is that it is controlling pleasure. That is to say, cells in the nucleus accumbens-dopamine system are active when we are taking or anticipating pleasure in some activity. There are several lines of evidence that seem to bear this out. In monkeys, cells in the nucleus accumbens start to fire up when a pleasant food is tasted, but also as soon as the monkey recognizes that food is going to be available. Moreover, almost all the major addictive drugs—cocaine, amphetamine, heroin, opium, and tobacco—have effects on dopamine-using cells. Cocaine, for example, deactivates an enzyme that breaks dopamine down, and thus causes extra dopamine to accumulate between neurons. Amphetamine causes extra dopamine to be released. Heroin, morphine and tobacco are slightly more indirect, operating on other chemical systems that in turn affect dopaminergic neurons, but their effects are still potent. And there is a surge of activity in the nucleus accumbens of the human male when he looks at a picture of an attractive female.

Perhaps most striking of all is the phenomenon known as 'brain stimulation reward'. When tiny electrodes are implanted into certain regions of the brain, animals become addicted to the electrical activity they can provide. Passing a small electric current through an area of the brain simulates—or exaggerates—the effects of that brain area being very active in normal brain functioning. There is one area in particular, the lateral hypothalamus, where rats or monkeys will do anything to get the electricity turned on. If the current is turned on intermittently, then other 'pleasure' behaviours such as eating or sex are increased. If the current is made to depend on pressing a lever, the animals will spend most of their time and energy on lever pressing. In fact, they will press the lever three thousand times to get a volley of stimulation. Working for this reward, they will ignore sexually receptive members of

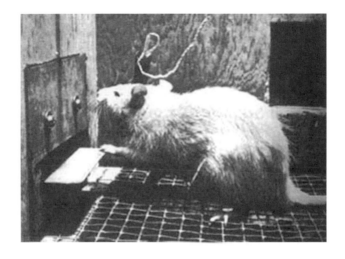

Fig. 5.1 Electric pleasure: A rat self-administering brain stimulation reward.

the opposite sex, food, or even water, in their single-minded quest for the hit.

This experiment is for obvious reasons difficult to replicate in humans, but it has been done. In the 1960s and 1970s, brain surgery was considered an option for severe epilepsy and other neurological conditions, and sometimes for psychiatric disorders too. Usually as a prelude to destroying or disconnecting particular regions of brain tissue, surgeons would implant tiny electrodes into different regions of the brain and pass electric current through them. An array of sub-cortical areas, generally the human equivalents of the rat mid-brain reward pathways, produced feelings of well-being when stimulated. The feelings ranged from the relief of anxiety, to curiosity, to general benevolent calm, to an euphoria described as close to orgasm. Patients allowed to self-administer the stimulation would do so just like the rats. Electrical stimulation of the brain is thus a possible avenue for the treatment of depression. Less invasive versions are being investigated. In transcranial magnetic stimulation, for example, coils are placed on the outside of the head, and these are used to induce electrical changes in brain tissue by creation of a magnetic field. There is no surgery or direct electric shock to the skull. The technique is in its infancy, but there is some evidence that it can be helpful in the treatment of depression.

The lateral hypothalamus, which is the main site of brain stimulation reward in the rat, connects directly to the nucleus accumbens dopamine system. In fact, rats will work just as hard at bar pressing in order to give themselves injections of dopamine straight into the nucleus accumbens as they will to give themselves electrical stimulation. Thus, it seems that this whole circuit is dedicated to controlling pleasurable behaviour. It seems as if the dopamine injection or electrical stimulation is mimicking the effect of doing something really fantastic. However, recent experiments show that something more interesting is going on.

With a little care, you can reliably judge how positive a rat's response to food is, by minutely observing behaviours as it takes the food. When it likes something, it laps and licks its paws. When it dislikes something, it shakes its head and rubs its face. When stimulation is applied to the lateral hypothalamus, the rat eats more, but its facial reaction shows that it doesn't enjoy it any more. Indeed, judging from the facial reactions, the animals actually *dislike* the food they are so motivated to seek. Conversely, when dopamine-blocking drugs are used to shut the system down, rats will starve even when surrounded by mountains of tasty food. However, if a sweet solution is diffused onto their tongues, their facial reactions show that they take the normal pleasure in the taste once it gets there. In other words, mechanisms that control the *wanting* of things are not identical to those that control the *liking* of them once they arrive. The two are after all logically quite distinct. You could crave for something very much, but take little or no pleasure in it once you had it.

There are examples from human psychology of the separation between wanting and liking. As we have seen, people are not very good at predicting the impact of attaining their desires on their feelings of happiness, imaging unrealistically large positive change when something sought after comes to pass. This may be because we confuse the fact that we want something with the assumption that we will therefore be happy when we get it. The drugs of abuse that act on dopamine systems all share the characteristic of being highly addictive, but not all of them are actually very enjoyable. Nicotine, for example, produces far too little pleasure for this to be a satisfactory account of why people are addicted to it. These drugs stimulate the wanting system, making them the perfect self-marketing products. If you are a smoker, you have been duped by chemistry into spending a lot of time and money on doing something you don't actually enjoy.

The dopamine system interacts with a class of brain chemicals called opioids, because of their similarity to opium (artificially made substances of this class are called opiates, whilst opioids are the natural ones). Opioids do seem to be directly involved in pleasure. They are released in the rat brain by sweet tastes. The injection of opiates into wide areas of the rat brain results in both more eating and more positive behaviours towards the food. And in humans, taking an opioid-blocking drug makes things that are usually delicious seem less so.

Drugs like heroin and morphine (opiates) mimic the body's own opioids, and this is thought to be the basis of the euphoria they produce. Opiates and opioids are also powerful painkillers. This is a very interesting phenomenon. As I argued in an earlier chapter, the function of positive emotions such as pleasure is to make you ignore conflicting demands and continue with an activity that is doing you good. Thus it makes sense to have opioids, which are released by a pleasurable activity, dampen down other signals that may be competing for your attention. When you are finally getting intimate with the mate of your dreams, you don't want to be thinking of food or your bruised knee. Magnify this effect up with an artificial opiate at hundreds of times natural concentrations, and you have morphine analgaesia.

Opioid and dopamine systems are reciprocally connected, and by the same token, wanting and liking usually go together. A recent study of hospitalized heroin addicts suggests how these interactions might work. The participants could work to receive an injection, which in some conditions was morphine and in some just saline solution. To get the solution, they had to press a lever three thousand times in 45 minutes. They also rated the injections they received, in terms of how much pleasure they gave, whether they thought the injection contained any drug, and so on. At moderate doses of morphine, participants rated the injections as pleasurable, and worked at lever pressing to get them. In the saline condition, they rated the injections as worthless and no good, and wouldn't press the lever. At a very low concentration of the drug, they still rated the injection worthless and no good, but they worked just as hard at lever pressing to get the solution injected as in the high-dose conditions. In other words, the low concentration did enough to activate the wanting system, but not enough to activate the liking system.

These drugs are all (magnified) mimics of our natural response to things that have been good for us over evolutionary time, like sex, good food, water, and escape from danger. The studies suggest that in the natural system too there could be interesting disconnections between desire and pleasure. Something that is strongly and directly fitness-enhancing like mating with someone one is attracted to is likely to do enough to activate both wanting and liking. Thus we will both feel good at the time and want to do it again (and somehow forget that we have a bruised knee, because of the opioid analgaesia). Something that is weakly fitness-enhancing, like for example, a slight rise in income or social status, might be a strong enough reward to engage the wanting system, but not enough to bring on the pleasure. This would account for the observation that we often work hard in life for things that turn out not to increase either pleasure or happiness. Like addicts, we somehow feel compelled to do so.

These studies have told us something about the brain basis of desire and pleasure, but, happiness is distinct from either of these. What soma produced was a feeling of calm, satisfaction, and well-being. This is where the serotonin system comes in.

As we saw, directly increasing serotonin activity in the brain through d-fenfluramine leads to a reduction in the type of thinking that goes with negative emotions such as worry and fear. Serotonin-enhancing drugs are effective in reducing depression, but also in reducing anxiety, phobias, and shyness. They can even be used to treat obsessive–compulsive disorder. This is a condition in which the person feels compelled to repeat certain thoughts and actions, such as checking rituals, or washing of the hands. This can be thought of in some respects as a type of anxiety, since often the person is worried about negative consequences that will ensue if the ritual is not done. Thus, the serotonin-boosting drugs seem able to disengage negative emotion systems. Similarly, studies have found evidence in the blood or brains of depressed, suicidal, and violent individuals that serotonin activity is unusually low.

So what is the serotonin system doing? This issue is not as yet entirely clear, but one possibility is that serotonin is the currency of particular brain circuits that modulate the balance between positive and negative emotions. Clearly, in life, positive and negative motivations need to be weighed up against one another, and the optimal balance depends on the context. A monkey finding fruit has a dilemma; how much effort to put into gorging himself and how much into looking out for predators. The optimal balance depends on the context. On open ground the negative systems should probably predominate, however tempting the morsel, whilst safe up a tree hedonism is the order of the day.

More importantly, the right balance of negative and positive emotions depends on the monkey. A low-ranking newcomer from outside the group has to be careful above all, because if he feasts he may get beaten up by the others. On the other hand, the alpha female can stroll in, fearing nothing from her sorority and relatively little from predators, since she will no doubt end up in the safest position at the centre of the troupe.

Serotonin-boosting drugs affect behaviour in precisely the way you would expect if they were shifting the relative weighting of the negative and positive emotion systems. They reduce worry, fear, panic, and sleeplessness. They increase sociability, co-operation and positive emotion. Most intriguingly, serotonin in wild monkeys has been shown to be related to social position. Low-ranking individuals have high levels of stress hormones and relatively low concentrations of blood serotonin. High-ranking individuals on the other hand, spend more time grooming, have lower stress hormones, and higher serotonin. And in a troupe with no alpha male, a subordinate given Prozac will rise to alpha status.

This puts a new perspective on the function of serotonin systems. It is tempting to think of the low-serotonin syndrome as simply a pathology, the brain going wrong. But in fact, the monkey studies suggest that it is based on a system that is adaptive. For the low-ranking monkeys, it is optimal to shift the balance towards the negative emotions. They have more to worry about, and if they are not careful, they will end up dead or ostracized from the group. Similarly, their high levels of stress are not a pathology as such. They need to reallocate resources from long-term problems such as social grooming and tissue repair to the immediate issues of remaining intact. Stress hormones mobilize the body's resources in this way.

There are some human parallels to this situation. Moving from one social group to another is very stress-ful, and new and insecure employees think in more paranoid ways than established and tenured ones. The lower people are on the socio-economic hierarchy, the higher they score on scales of anxiety and depression. In part they are right to do so: they have more to worry about. Long-term health is potently affected by social status, even though the advances in medicine and wealth of the last few decades mean that the poorest people today have objective conditions much better than the richest of a few generations ago. But having the most insecure place in society is still a potent initi-ator of a serotonergically mediated shift from positive, low-stress mode to negative, high-stress mode.

At the extreme of the low-serotonin spectrum are the

clinical disorders of negative emotion, namely depression and anxiety disorder. There is some debate about whether these are simply an extreme of the adaptive range, or whether in these cases the mechanism really has gone wrong. I tend to favour the latter possibility, since the long-term hopelessness, destruction and passivity of clinical depression seem unlikely to be related to anything that could be beneficial. It could be that what happens is that mechanisms that could have been adaptive for brief bouts in our ancestors (sit tight and don't do anything) become instead chronically activated in some people, to the point where they are pathologies. Antidepressants and psychotherapy are ways of trying to disengage this activation.

If this view of the serotonin system's function is correct, then we should be able to make some predictions about drugs of abuse that mimic a serotonin shot. First, they should produce more of a relaxed, disinhibited sense of well-being than the euphoria rush of cocaine or heroin. Second, they should not be directly addictive in the way that the dopamine drugs are, since they are not operating primarily on the wanting system, but on the system that shifts away from negative emotions to positive ones. Of course, addiction could still occur, but it would be indirect—i.e. via the positive feelings induced—rather than chemically direct.

Such a drug exists, and its name is, aptly enough, Ecstasy. Ecstasy, whose active ingredient is a chemical called MDMA, has a very illuminating history. A powerful releaser of serotonin, it was first synthesized many decades ago, but did not immediately find a niche. In the psychedelic 1960s and 1970s, its use was seriously advocated as adjunct to psychotherapy. This is because it produces a powerful feeling of well-being, insight, and compassion. In the 1980s, it began to spread seriously as a recreational drug, associated with an expanding and vibrant dance culture. It was criminalized in the 1980s, but this only seems to have accelerated its spread, with millions of tablets being taken every weekend across the developed world.

Ecstasy, lacking the hungriness of the desire-driven opiates, and promoting harmony and solidarity amongst its party-going users, might seem like a dream narcotic. However, the hang-over began in the 1990s. MDMA causes damage to brain cells in experimental animals, and soon evidence began to accumulate of memory impairments in users of Ecstasy. Moreover, though the drug provides a short-term boost in serotonergic transmission, it leaves the opposite effect as it wears off. By mid-week, regular users show evidence of low mood, depression, and aggression, dispelled, presumably, only by the next weekend's dose.

There is another class of serotonin-related drugs: the hallucinogens, such as LSD. LSD is chemically related to serotonin. It is not just modern chemists who have discovered the psychological significance of serotonin. Indigenous peoples in many locations have refined compounds resembling serotonin from sources as diverse as cactus (mescaline), mushrooms (psilocybin), and the vine that gives native South Americans aya-huasca. The effects of these drugs are somewhat different from those of Ecstasy, with a greater emphasis on hallucination, but the feeling of expansiveness and self-transcendence is shared. Among native Ecuadorians and Peruvians, there is a tradition of using ayahuasca in the contexts of healing, self-discovery, worship, and shamanism, and LSD, too, was experimented with in the context of psychotherapy.

The modulation of positive and negative emotion systems seems also in part to be a modulation between the left and right sides of the brain. Recall that a circuit including the amygdala seems to be responsible for the emotional tagging of experiences. The amygdala further connects to areas of the frontal lobes. When smiling in response to an amusing film clip, subjects show enhanced brain activity across the left hemisphere, and reduced activity across the right, compared to when they are reacting to a disgusting clip. When volunteers in PET studies were made to feel sad by watching a film clip or being asked to generate sad memories, one locus of increased activation was in the right frontal cortex, and the same finding has come from comparing depressed patients with normal volunteers with the brain at rest.

Similarly, the relative strength of left and right frontal brain activation before an experiment has begun is a good predictor of the way a person will respond to an emotional experience. People with an excess of left hemisphere activity will respond in a strongly positive way to positive film clips, whereas people with an excess of right hemisphere activity will respond in a strongly negative way to negative ones. Thus, the balance of activity in the brain at rest must reflect the person's emotional 'preset', which is presumably in turn controlled by serotonergic circuits. This would seem to lead to the hypothesis, untested to my knowledge, that d-fenfluramine or an SSRI should shift the balance brain activation from the right to the left frontal lobes.

A recent study by Melissa Rosenkrantz and her colleagues further demonstrated the significance of brain lop-sidedness. The researchers established the lateral bias of frontal brain activation at rest, and then injected their particpants with influenza vaccine. Vaccines are partially disabled forms of disease bugs, but the immune system does not know that they are disabled and attacks them just as it would the real thing. Indeed, this is why vaccination is effective. Rosenkrantz found that the higher the levels of right frontal brain activation at rest, the less effective, in terms of the amount of antibody produced, the person's immune response was to the vaccine.

This fascinating finding fills in some of the missing links between happiness and health. Habitual emotional state is a predictor of long-term health and life expectancy, and neuroticism and depression are associated with poor physical as well as psychological health outcomes. However, there are still many unknown steps in the pathway between the body and mind, as it were. Now it seems that general emotional state, determined in part by asymmetry of frontal brain activation, controls the magnitude of the stress response. Stress is a system controlled by hormones that essentially shifts investment between short-term and long-term goals. Under stress, blood is diverted from gut to muscles, sugar and adrenaline are released, and non-urgent functions are damped down. This is fine—indeed, very helpful—for a short burst of running from a predator— but if the system is engaged all the time, long-term health problems are bound to result. Unhappiness, anxiety and depression engage the stress system pathologically, leading to suppression of the immune system. This must be the key to their negative long-term consequences.

We saw in the previous chapter that personality factors powerfully affect levels of positive and negative emotion in life. These personality factors must reflect some aspect of how the individual is wired up, and so you should be able to find differences in the brains of, for example, introverts and extroverts.

The first prediction you would make on the basis of the material reviewed so far is that individuals high in neuroticism should show a relatively strong activation of right frontal areas of the brain, whilst those high in extroversion should show strong activation on the left. There are some studies that suggest this may be the case. Richard Davidson and colleagues of the University of Wisconsin observed play sessions amongst young toddlers. They were able to classify the youngsters into relatively inhibited and uninhibited individuals, on the basis of things like staying close to mother, trying out new toys, talkativeness, and so on. They later showed that the inhibited children, whilst at rest, had relatively greater right side activation, and the uninhibited ones greater activity on the left. This effect could not be put down to the particular mood of the children that day, since the brain activity measurements were taken several months after the observations of behaviour. Similarly, as we have seen, brain activity asymmetry *before* an emotional challenge predicts the type of response the person will give, suggesting that asymmetry is picking up stable aspects of the individual's personality, rather than just their current state.

The second prediction that we might make about personality is that there will be a relationship between the functioning of the serotonin and dopamine systems and the individual's personality characteristics. If the serotonin system mediates the balance between positive and negative emotions, then one might expect that high neuroticism, which is the tendency to favour negative emotions, would be associated with some change in serotonin system function. There is evidence for this prediction. There is a gene called 5HTT, which is involved in building the serotonin system (it actually regulates the production of a protein that removes serotonin from the synapse as it is used in passing messages between neurons). This gene has two common forms, a short one and a long one. People with at least one copy of the long form of this gene have, on average, lower neuroticism scores than people with two copies of the short form.

On the other hand, we argued in the last chapter that

extroversion could be understood as an enhancement of wanting the good things in life. In this case, dopamine functioning might be altered in some way. Here again there is some evidence, though it is probably fair to say that the case is not proven as yet. The gene that creates one type of receptor for brain dopamine comes in multiple forms. Some studies have suggested that the longer the forms of the gene a person is carrying, the higher will be their score on personality dimensions like extroversion.

These findings are very exciting. We are at last beginning to understand how genes make bits of brain, and how bits of brain make feelings and behaviour. However, they could also be seen as a bit bleak. If happiness is determined by chemical reactions, which are in part determined by a genetic blueprint, then what hope is there, short of drugging myself or attempting genetic engineering, of ever becoming happier? In short, can happiness be changed? This is the subject of the next chapter.

6

Panaceas and placebos

I t might be tempting to conclude, from the material surveyed thus far, that there is nothing much to be done about happiness. Of course, you can boost it for a few hours by going to a party, eating chocolate, or having sex, but these pleasures will fade and you will be back where you started. Larger life changes, however apparently desirable, are subject to adaptation in a few weeks or months. Personality factors, which are rather set for life, are strong determinants of basic happiness. Finally, we are beginning to understand that brain functioning is in direct control of our happiness.

We should not be too overawed by this last finding. Of course brain functioning was going to turn out to be in direct control of our happiness—how could it be otherwise? Did we expect happiness to be controlled by a muscle in our feet? It was just a question of how long it took to find out how it worked. But the brain is a supremely flexible organ that changes its chemistry in adaptive response to what is going on around it. Finding out that something has a brain basis doesn't make it intrinsically any more or less malleable by psychological or social means.

There are evidently people out there who want us to believe that it is possible to change happiness. A visit to the local book shop will yield a whole shelf of felicity panaceas (there are 2000 new self-help titles a year), possibly including the following:

DANCE NAKED IN YOUR LIVING ROOM

CHANGE YOUR UNDERWEAR, CHANGE YOUR LIFE

BOLDLY LIVE AS YOU NEVER LIVED BEFORE: LIFE LESSONS FROM STAR TREK.

Happiness solutions on sale are not restricted to books. There is a plethora of therapies, alternative therapies, herbal products, alternative herbal products, spiritual systems, alternative spiritual systems, etc., etc. Plus, of course, advertising in general works by showing happy people happily using the latest material trinket. Most of these solutions are untested or even untestable, yet the uptake of these products is simply astounding. They range from the common sense and helpful, via those which work at best through some kind of placebo effect, to the depths of quackery and charlatanism.

Such research as has been carried out suggests that many people find self-help books and other self-administered therapies helpful. This research, though, is mainly concentrated at the more sensible end of the market. The possible downside in terms of the unrealistic expectations that are raised has not been systematically investigated. This is a real issue, though. Many of the books available seem to suggest that we can all become supermen and women, with no problems, perfect happiness, and limitless wealth and energy. Simply reading the back jackets of some of these books is enough to make one feel inadequate. And if we read them and remain our everyday selves with limited energy and a routine life, what then? Is there something wrong with us?

Our intuitive feeling that there is *some way* of being perfectly happy often makes us credulous when it comes to these therapies and systems. Like players of lotteries, we seem to concede that objective considerations show that it is extremely unlikely that there is a simple way of reaching everlasting bliss, but as soon as we think about ourselves, we wonder if it might just work. There might just be something in it. If we just gave it a try .... This endearing and irrational optimism is of course the marketing executive's dream.

The whole genre of happiness panaceas seems to rest

on twin assumptions; first, that personal happiness can be increased, and second, that increased personal happiness is what people want. Other things being equal, the latter is a reasonably accurate claim, though the situation is often more complex, as we shall see in the next chapter. However, it is undoubtedly true that people *think* they want to increase personal happiness and *hate it* when they suspect someone else is getting more happiness than they are. This makes 'Increases your happiness!' a potent and vital strapline to stick on to your advertising somewhere, even if your product actually does something quite different and does it well. But what about the evidence that these things can actually have any effect?

Actually, and perhaps surprisingly given some of the findings that have been reviewed thus far, there is quite a lot of evidence that happiness can be deliberately manipulated, with measurable if modest effects. Though personality may predispose an individual to a certain set of emotional norms, deliberate interventions can limit the impact of emotional reactions in ways that make a lot of difference. The most-studied non-drug interventions are the various forms of psychotherapy, and for depression, the best psychotherapy is about equally effective as antidepressants. (The optimal strategy will often be the combination of the two.) However, self-help books and videos, and happiness training pro-grammes, which are often intellectually modelled on psychotherapy, also yield effects. Finally, evidence for the positive impact of practices such as meditation is mounting.

None of these solutions is miraculous, and perhaps the best therapy of all is the realization that total happi-ness is neither an attainable nor the only important aspiration. However, there are three kinds of psycho-logical changes that deliberate manipulation can bring about. The first is reducing the impact of negative emo-tion; the second, increasing positive emotion; and the third I shall call changing the subject.

An excess of the negative emotions—fear, worry, sad-ness, anger, guilt, shame—is one of the most potent causes of unhappiness. These emotions have a pecu-liarly imperialistic quality. If we have been rejected by one lover, we easily start to think that no-one will ever find us attractive. If we feel guilty for not looking after a relative better, guilt at all kinds of other things we have done may start to creep in. If we are upset that some-thing at work has gone wrong, it is easy to feel that it can never be repaired, and that everything we ever do there will go wrong.

The negative emotions are very different from the

positive ones in this regard. If we win a darts match, we do not generally start to imagine we will win at everything we do. If someone is unexpectedly nice to us, we do not tend to imagine that everyone will now be nice to us, or at least, not to the same extent as the converse if someone is unexpectedly horrible to us. The origin of this asymmetry is the different functions of the positive and negative emotions. The negative emotions function as essentially emergency responses in situations which are bad for our fitness and which should not be repeated too often. The positive emotions simply tag something which is good for us and say, keep doing this for the time being. Thus, negative emotions are more urgent and capture consciousness in a much more total way.

An illustration of this principle in animal behaviour is what is known as the life/dinner problem. When a cheetah runs after a gazelle, which of the two should run for longer? The gazelle is running for its life, so it should keep running until well after the point where it starts to adversely affect its long-term health. In fact, it should run until a point just before it will drop dead of exhaustion, since that would be no worse than what will happen anyway if it stops earlier. The cheetah on the other hand is running for its dinner. It should stop running at some much earlier point, since another potential dinner is likely to wander past in the next few hours anyway.

Let us assume that the gazelle experiences fear when the cheetah launches its attack. From the gazelle's perspective, it needs the fear program to motivate it to keep running to the end, to devote all resources to running however much the muscles protest, to treat the situation as essentially catastrophic, because if it stops, it would be a catastrophe. The cheetah, on the other hand, is presumably motivated by desire. From the cheetah's perspective, you would want the desire program to keep it running for a while, but be prepared to stop if it felt a bit stiff, because there is no point getting lame for a plate of gazelle-tartare.

The evolutionary legacy of this asymmetry is that negative emotion systems are potent at capturing our full consciousness and invading all our thoughts, long after the equivalent positive ones would have given up and faded away. For example, we lie awake at night full of anxiety about some situation we can do nothing about anyway; and in the process we make ourselves anxious about other situations too. Alternatively, we ruminate on the shame of a particularly crass thing we did, and it makes us believe that everything we do is foolish and no-one will ever respect us again.

These thoughts, however, are essentially irrational.

The things in modern life that cause us fear, shame, and sadness are really—by and large—not as threatening as a large carnivore. No-one, in Western societies at least, dies of starvation. The homicide rate is very low. Our social groups are very fluid and flexible, so if we fall out with the people in one social network, we will find others. Thus our negative emotion programs, designed as they were to cope with real, ugly, Palaeolithic emergencies, go off on a needless rumination of fear and worry. This becomes a self-fulfilling prophecy, since our constant fear and worry makes us more hostile, more paranoid, less attractive, and less open to good things that might come along.

The approach known as cognitive-behavioural therapy (CBT) works on this insight to reduce negative thoughts and feelings. Therapist and client work to identify patterns of negative thinking, and expose their irrationality. For example, depressed people often have automatic negative thoughts, recurrent ideas that pop into their heads that have no real basis. By identifying what they are, and discussing their baselessness, the client can counter their impact on mood when they arise. Negative emotions also make us exaggerate—for example, not wanting to tell someone something because of their potential anger, when in fact the worst that can happen is that they will be angry and then the world will continue to turn—and catastrophize—that is, assume that because one thing goes wrong everything we do is disastrous. CBT carefully probes these kinds of thoughts, identifying where the distortions and false inferences lie, and provides counter arguments. The therapy is in a way a conversation between the siren voices of negative emotions systems and our more rational, analytic cognitive resources. The thing is that negative emotion systems, and other automatic tics we have like comparing what we have with what others have, may be optimally designed from the point of view of natural selection, but not optimally designed from the point of view of life. For one thing, they were designed for a world of real physical danger, high mortality, and small, impossible to escape social groups. Thus, they tend to exaggerate fear, shame, and the risk of social ostracism. Moreover, natural selection doesn't, in Randolph Nesse's memorable phrase, give a fig for our happiness. It just wants us alive and making babies, miserably if need be.

On the other hand, natural selection has also provided us with a multi-level mind, in which relatively automatic emotion programs can be modulated by information from context, planning, logic, further reflection, and so on. CBT amplifies this modulation by providing a rational therapist to prod and suggest.

Though there is some debate about both the effectiveness of CBT and why it actually works, the weight of opinion is that it is very useful in the treatment of depression, anxiety, and associated problems. Indeed, it has recently been shown that a 15–20 session course changes patterns of brain activity, though interestingly in a different way from antidepressant drugs. Programs to increase happiness in the non-depressed population, and many good self-help books, incorporate some CBT insights and techniques. The strength of CBT is that it doesn't require you to change anything about your material circumstances, or even what you do day-to-day. It certainly does not stop negative feelings coming up; it merely stops them spiralling into a self-fulfilling prophecy of stress and alienation. The key is simply to start thinking differently about things.

Cognitive behavioural therapy, even if successful, does not make you more happy so much as less unhappy. That is, eliminating the excessive effects of negative emotions might move you from unhappy to neutral, but will not take you to the positive end of the range. In certain ways, that may be enough. The negative emotions are peculiarly debilitating and can stop you attaining any kind of perspective and direction in life. A slight lack of pleasure, on the other hand, doesn't stop you getting on with things if you have other sources of direction in life. However, happiness training programmes do also aim to increase positive emotion.

Such increase is generally achieved by pleasant activity training. This staggeringly complex technique consists of determining which activities are pleasant, and doing them more often. You could rely on your intuitions about which things you like, and then make a list of them, and resolve to do them more often. Alternatively, you could be really scientific, and keep a log of all the things you do each day, and a separate log of your mood, over several weeks. You could then perform a statistical analysis of the data, to see which activities were reliably associated with better moods. The kinds of things that generally surface from such analyses are seeing friends, sports, cultural activities, going out, and visiting new places.

Pleasant activity training is one way of relieving depression, and furthermore, when applied to non-depressed volunteers over several weeks, also improves their ratings of happiness. In the latter case, it does raise an immediate question: if, as is generally assumed, pleasure makes people do things more often whilst pain makes them avoid them, then why aren't they already doing the pleasant things in life as often as they reasonably can anyway? How could it possibly be the case that something so simple as asking people to do pleasant things more often would make them happier, and why hadn't they long ago discovered this for themselves?

The answer may be to question whether people's decisions are really driven by happiness, or at any rate, by pleasure. The distinction between wanting and liking is of use here. Our minds are equipped with a dopamine-drunk wanting system that draws us to compete for a promotion or a higher salary; a larger house or more material goods; an attractive partner or 2.4 children. It draws us to these things, not because they will make us happy, not even because we like them, though some of them we do, but because the ancestors who got the stone age equivalents of these things are our ancestors, and those who did not are biological dead ends. Although we implicitly feel that the things we want in life will make us happy, this may be a particularly cruel trick played by our evolved mind to keep us competing. The things we want in life are the things the evolved mind tells us to want, and it doesn't give a fig about our happiness. All the evidence suggests that you would probably be happier not caring about your promotion and going and building boats or doing volunteer work instead. Moreover, the more important people believe financial success is, the more dissatisfied with both work and family life they are.

This means, rather surprisingly, that it is quite possible that people could be so preoccupied with wanting things that they could forget to do things they enjoy. Naturally this will make them dissatisfied, though they will quite possibly be successful in life by all orthodox (and evolutionary) criteria. People's behaviour is driven by desire, and by an implicit theory about what will make them happy. This implicit theory may be at odds with what is really the case. Recall that people over-estimate how much happier achieving the things they want will make them, and under-estimate their ability to cope with things that they don't want. Learning from experience is not guaranteed to sort these kinds of errors out, because the design of the implicit theory is not to improve personal contentment but to replicate the person's DNA.

However, through techniques such as pleasant activities training, you can, in principle at least, avoid the pitfall of the system of desire that usually motivates behaviour. Both pleasant activities training and CBT have a very interesting implication. We tend to assume that our unhappiness is the result of other people's hostile actions, or corporate capital (for socialists), or the state (for conservatives), or God (for atheists) or Mammon (for believers). Actually, however, it appears more likely that chronic unhappiness is the result of mechanisms internal to ourselves, be it the tyranny of wanting rather than liking, or the hyperactivity of negative emotions. Moreover, it is not that unhappiness is the result of mechanisms within ourselves that have gone wrong. The wanting system is *supposed* to enslave you, to make you maximize your reproductive success. The negative emotion system is *supposed* to be hyperactive, because suffering ten false alarms is better than getting killed. Thus our biggest enemy, if we decide we want to be happy beings, is the very psychology we have to use to do it. Fortunately, however, that psychology is pretty smart and pretty flexible, and so can come up with ruses like CBT and pleasant activities training to have a dialogue with itself.

This brings us to the last and perhaps most potent way that we can intervene to affect happiness: that is, changing the subject. CBT and pleasant activities training are both ways of manipulating the hedonic quality of life, via thoughts in the one case, and activities in the other. But focusing inwards on hedonic experience is not the only possible strategy. Indeed, doing so opens up the danger of what has long been known as the 'hedonic paradox'. The hedonic paradox is the notion that by pursuing happiness itself, one makes it more distant, whereas by pursuing something else, one can inadvertently bring it closer. The paradox was clearly articulated by, amongst others, John Stuart Mill:

> Those only are happy . . . who have their minds fixed on some object other than their own happiness. Aiming thus at something else, they find happiness along the way.

By contrast, by focusing in on one's own happiness, one inevitably draws attention to its shortfall; 'ask yourself whether you are happy, and you cease to be so.'

Throughout the ages, people have sought to minimize the impact of negative emotions by connecting to things larger than themselves. Many people find nature, and the grandeur of natural landscapes, a tonic in this way. Indeed, it has even been suggested that our craving for expansive, open landscapes with water and wildlife represents the vestiges of a mechanism for seeking out the kinds of places in which the lives of our ancestors flourished. We are also connected to things beyond ourselves by people's stories, not just the real stories of our friends, but the imaginary stories told in art and literature. Such narratives reflect back to us that we are not alone in having faced the complex task of being a human being. Others find intrinsic satisfaction in organizing and intervening in the physical world, be it collecting stamps or building kites.

Religious faith also connects people to something beyond themselves. There is plenty of evidence that people who practice religion enjoy benefits in health and well-being. However, there are several possible explanations. One is that religious groups provide social support and connectedness, whilst another is in terms of the kind of personalities who tend to become religious. Moreover, religions tend to promote healthy lifestyles. However, another possible factor is a cognitive one: the meta-narrative of religion reduces anxiety about the travails of existence, and consoles the individual with a larger context for his or her thoughts and feelings.

The Yale psychologist Patricia Linville has shown that individuals vary in the complexity of their self-image. For example, I can think of myself as just an academic, or as an academic, writer, teacher, cook, friend, badminton player and so on. Linville has found that the more complex a person's self-image is, the less their happiness in life swings up and down when they do well or badly at something. The reason is very clear; if I am just an academic, and I have an academic setback, then my whole self seems less efficacious and worthwhile. However, if I have many other facets to myself, then the effect of the setback on my identity is much less severe. Linville's studies show that self-complexity helps avoid symptoms of depression when a person is under stress. Similarly, people who belong to community organizations, do voluntary work, and have rich social connections are healthier and happier than those who do not.

Focusing on a wider set of concerns doesn't necessarily mean that suffering is any less real. It does, however, put our feelings into context. Another technique that does this is meditation. The evidence of a positive effect of meditation on subjective well-being is becoming quite impressive. Regular meditators have reduced levels of negative emotion, and a course of mindfulness meditation in volunteers has been shown to reduce stress, increase well-being and improve immune responses. Mindfulness meditation teaches people to become aware of the contents of their consciousness but able to detach themselves from it. Thus negative emotions can be seen in context for what they are: bothersome, but transitory, and not an integral part of the person experiencing them. This principle is also used in a recently developed version of cognitive therapy, mindfulness-based cognitive therapy. Whereas in CBT the emphasis is on changing and combating negative thoughts, in mindfulness-based cognitive therapy, the emphasis is more on simply becoming aware of the contents of consciousness and being able to observe it non-judgementally, thus achieving some detachment from the impact of negative thoughts.

Interestingly, a large body of work over the last two decades has shown that writing regularly about one's experiences clearly has beneficial effects on well-being and health. It even makes a measurable difference to immune function. Writing seems to have its healing effects whether the experiences written about are negative or positive ones. Thus the explanation is not as simple as a venting of otherwise pent up negative thoughts. I suspect that writing itself allows us to become more mindful of our thoughts, and at the same time take distance from them, replicating in a way the effects of mindfulness therapy or meditation.

Along with detaching oneself from pain is detaching oneself from desire. As we saw in Chapter 5, human beings are powerfully driven by systems of desire, which become attached to material possessions and social status. The gap between these desires and what the world can reasonably yield is an enduring source of frustration. We have already seen that the more importance people place on money, the less satisfied they are with their income. One important way of changing the subject may be to give up on desires and wants that either cannot be fulfilled, or which remain insatiable despite their continual feeding. William James pointed out how such relinquishing can be a tonic:

> To give up pretensions is as blessed a relief as to get them gratified. There is a strange lightness in the heart when one's nothingness in a particular area is accepted in good faith. How pleasant is the day when we give up striving to be young or slender. 'Thank God' we say, 'Those illusions are gone!'

The relinquishing of desires is a feature of Stoic philosophy, and a recurrent aspect of many religious traditions. In Christianity, detachment from desire is usually advocated on the grounds of morals, not morale, but it may be psychologically beneficial as a way of weaning people off insatiable and thus ultimately self-defeating appetites, particularly in the material realm. In the East, there is a long tradition of voluntary simplicity and the attempt to manage desires skilfully. In Buddhism, happiness depends on the mind, not on external trappings. There is a well-known joke about a rich American visitor who goes to see the Dalai Lama in his mountain retreat in India. He takes a huge gift-wrapped parcel for his host. The Tibetan sage hesitantly undoes the gaudy wrapping, but the box proves to be completely empty. 'Ah' gasps the Dalai Lama, 'Exactly what I've always wanted!'

Just as materialism breeds dissatisfaction with material conditions, constantly aspiring to find happiness in doing or having can make it more difficult to be happy. As Keats suggested, to experience happiness requires us to be at least sometimes fully present in the here and now, and not distracted by desires or self-consciousness:

> It is a flaw
> In happiness, to see beyond our bourn—
> It forces us in summer skies to mourn
> It spoils the singing of the nightingale.

7

A design for living

[Life] is an endless, truly endless struggle. There's no time when we are going to arrive at a plateau where the whole thing gets sorted. It's a struggle in the way every plant has to find its own way to stand up straight. A lot of the time it's a failure. And yet it's not a failure if some enlightenment comes from it.

ARTHUR MILLER

In *Mostly harmless*, the fifth book in the alarmingly inaccurately named *Hitchhiker's guide to the galaxy* trilogy, the late Douglas Adams recounts the story of the development of intelligent robots at a research institute called MISPWOSO (the Maximegalon Institute of Slowly and Painfully Working Out the Surprisingly Obvious). Robots can be made intelligent to a point by giving them more and more specific sets of instructions for what to do under different circumstances. The problem with this approach is that the robots, to do anything interesting, have to be pre-programmed with millions and millions of lines of code, and are still completely stuffed whenever any situation arises that their programmer had not thought of ahead of time.

The MISPWOSO breakthrough came when they gave their robots the capacity to be happy. Vast wodges of computer code could now be scrapped. All the programmers needed to do was to give the robots (a) the capacity for happiness or unhappiness; (b) some simple conditions that needed to be satisfied in order to bring these states about; and (c) the capacity to learn from experience. The robots would then figure out what to do for themselves.

As so often with science fiction, there is a serious insight here, and it is not about imaginary robots, but about the architecture of real people. The psychological equivalent of the MISPWOSO hypothesis would be the following. We are a supremely flexible species that has made it, living in diverse ways and fluid contexts. There is no way that evolution could have given us specific innate instructions for what to do in every possible situation that we might encounter. Instead, to a very considerable extent, it devolved responsibility to the environment, saying things like, pick up the social norms and best behavioural strategies of the people you find yourself amongst. Most importantly, it gave us the capacity for happiness, and a few simple conditions for eliciting this state. These conditions have been produced by natural selection because in the ancestral environment they would have all been positively correlated with reproductive success. First, be happier if you are physically and materially secure than if you are not; second, be happier if you have a mate than not; third, be happier if you have high social status than low, and so on. How to actually attain the happiness conditions is not specified, but it does not need to be. By making happiness a positive state, and providing a learning ability that will increase behaviours leading to positive outcomes and decrease behaviours leading to negative ones, the optimal behaviour of the individual has been assured.

In fact, the MISPWOSO idea is a rather accurate picture of how psychologists have traditionally thought human motivation works. Though the idea is not so very wrong, the material reviewed in this book allows us to see that the system we have been endowed with is rather more sophisticated, and needs to be so for good evolutionary reasons.

The problem with the MISPWOSO design for living is that the conditions for happiness it uses are absolute. The idea is that we are endowed with rules like 'If you have a mate, be happy'. The problem with this is that evolution is an inherently competitive process, and reproductive success is always relative to others in the environment. It is true that having a mate would give a man higher reproductive success than men around him with no mates. However, if he was living in a polygamous context where some men had three or four, then he would be at the bottom of the evolutionary pile. The same rule applies even more strongly to material conditions. Having a safe, dry cave might be great when one's competitors are roaming the dark woods, but when they are living in brick houses with dishwashers, it is probably not such a clever strategy.

Thus, at the very least, evolution would need to provide us with a context-specific anchoring for our happiness conditions. In other words, we would need to come equipped with a rule that says something like, look at the people around you, and be happy to the extent that you are doing better than them in the domains of health, material conditions, and mating.

Even this might not be enough. The MISPWOSO idea is that once the conditions for happiness have been met, the robot just keeps on doing whatever it has done to get it there. The problem with this is that the environment is full of possibilities. This berry patch could be great, but the salmon migration could be beginning in the stream over the other side of the hill. An individual too happy in her berry patch might be disadvantaged relative to her competitors, since she would be last into the salmon run. Therefore evolution should (a) never make us completely happy, or not for long; and (b) make us quickly adapt to the baseline of the best thing we have at the moment, and focus on the possibility of getting something better in the future, even if we don't know what that is yet.

The converse side of this relative happiness anchoring is that there is no particular point being too unhappy, especially when others around are doing no better. As we have seen, states of extreme unhappiness are emergency physiological responses. They mobilize energy to the muscles and brain while cutting investment to the immune system and tissue repair. These strategies should really be retained for short-term use. If the environment is unpropitious in the longer term, but cannot be changed, an organism would do better by getting used to it, and eking out what life it can. Thus, you would expect the evolution of rules that say, in effect, if the environment is difficult but cannot be changed and affects everyone else just as badly, turn off the extreme unhappiness. If something really and permanently bad for fitness happens, use the emergency responses, but damp them down over time and return to the set point.

This viewpoint makes sense of many of the findings

reviewed in this book. Here is a recapitulation of some of the main ones.

- The vast majority of people say they are more happy than unhappy. This is true even in poor countries and amongst poorer social groups in rich ones, and true amongst the unemployed, bereaved, and disabled.
- Very few people say they are completely happy. Most people think they will be even happier in the future than they are now.
- Happiness with domains like income and material goods is relative to what others around are getting.
- People adapt quite quickly to positive changes in life circumstances, and then return to close to their previous level of happiness.
- People become very unhappy after seriously negative life events like injury or divorce, but in most cases there is substantial adaptation to the new conditions.

There are, however, a number of findings that require still further revision of the model. For one thing, as we have seen, people are really not very good at predicting what the effect of their choices on their happiness will be. Moreover, they are prepared to work hard, in the laboratory and in life, for things that they don't actually enjoy very much, and sometimes need to be trained to do things that are pleasant. None of this makes sense if our psychology is designed for the attainment of happiness.

Instead, it seems that evolution has endowed us with several different systems relevant to happiness. One is the pleasure system. Its currency is opioids, and its operation is short term. The purpose of this system seems to be to turn off all competing demands and other possible activities whilst a bout of something good for fitness is completed. Pleasure is triggered by such obviously beneficial outcomes as love, sex, esteem, food. Pleasure soon fades, of course, as those activities satisfy the relevant appetites, or competing demands impinge.

On the other hand, we have a system of desire. This system is run by mid-brain dopamine circuits. It motivates us to work long hours for things like pay rises and status goods. It shapes behaviour on a long-term basis. Whilst many of the things we desire will also give pleasure, it is not necessary that they do so, since the two systems are partially independent. Thus, rather than making us desire to be happy, evolution has made us desire things that are generally good for our fitness. We evolved in an environment where status was highly correlated with reproductive success, and material resources were always scarce. Thus our motivational psychology tells us to compete for status and to acquire resources. We might think we want to do this because it will make us happy. Actually, we want to do it because our most successful ancestors were the ones who wanted to, and the bit about happiness is a kind of mirage.

Evolution has given us a strong implicit theory of happiness. That is, we come to the world believing that there is such a thing as achievable happiness, that it is desirable and important, and that the things that we desire will bring it about. It is not self-evident that any of these are actually true. This does not matter, however. Evolution's purposes are served if it can trick us in to working for things that are good for our fitness. It can do this by making us believe that those things bring happiness, and that happiness is what we want. It doesn't actually have to deliver the happiness in the end. The idea of happiness has done its job if it has kept us trying. In other words, evolution hasn't set us up for the attainment of happiness, merely its pursuit. It says, there's a crock of gold at the end of this next rainbow, and when we get to the end it says, there's a crock of gold at the end of this next rainbow. We don't necessarily learn from experience that this is a trick, because we are not necessarily designed to do so. It is in this sense that Immanuel Kant was right to say that the concept of happiness is a construct not of reason, but of the imagination.

This view makes sense of many of the other findings reviewed through the book.

- People are fascinated by the idea of happiness, and will follow any system that seems to promise it, despite evidence that there are other goods in life. Systems for living that are actually promising something else, like flow, solidarity, or autonomy, often have to sell their product on a happiness ticket as a marketing ploy.
- Wanting and liking are partly dissociable. Recall the morphine experiment where addicts would work for a low dose of morphine, but not enjoy it when it came (Chapter 5).
- We make many behavioural choices, like putting in long hours for pay rises and promotions, that probably bring no pleasure. We would, in all likelihood, attain more enjoyment by trading income or material goods for time with people or hobbies, but most people do not do so.
- People make quite inaccurate judgements about the effect of goal attainment on their happiness, over-estimating the positive effect of desired things, and

underestimating their ability to adjust to undesired things.
- People sometimes require training to make them do things that they actually enjoy.

In his play *Man and superman*, George Bernard Shaw has one of his characters exclaim: 'A lifetime of happiness! No man alive could bear it: it would be hell on earth.' This points up one of the many fascinating paradoxes associated with happiness. Although we all seem to feel that happiness is desirable and its pursuit important, fictional worlds where everyone is happy are never Utopias. In fact, they are always dystopias against which people rebel. Even the one example that I can find that was offered as a Utopia, B. F. Skinner's *Walden two*, is felt by many subsequent readers to be a nightmare vision.

The finest example is Huxley's *Brave new world*. It is hard at first to pinpoint why the England Huxley gives us is a dystopia. There are concerns about the level of state manipulation of individual lives (actually corporate manipulation, since the state and big corporations have essentially fused). However, most arguments against institutional interventions in individual lives are premised on the notion that such interventions make people unhappy. But everyone is happy in Huxley's world. It is true that their consciousnesses are dulled by drugs, but again, the usual objection to dulling one's consciousness is that it leads to unhappiness, and soma does not do this. So what basis is there to object to Huxley's world?

As the novel goes on, it becomes clear what is missing. What Huxley offers us is a world with happiness but no *flow*. Flow, you will recall, is a state where challenges are high, but skills are sufficient to match them. It is not necessarily a happy state, but it is a fulfilling and gripping one. In *Brave new world*, bland consumerism, social engineering, entertainment, and drugs mean that all conceivable pleasures are available with essentially zero effort or possibility of failure. Thus speaks the Controller of Western Europe:

> 'Consider your own likes' said Mustapha Mond. 'Has any of you ever encountered an insurmountable obstacle?'
> The question was answered by a negative silence.
> 'Has any of you been compelled to live through a long time-interval between a desire an its fulfilment?'
> 'Well,' began one of the boys .... 'I once had to wait nearly four weeks before a girl I wanted would let me have her.'
> 'And you felt a strong emotion in consequence?'
> 'Horrible!'
> 'Horrible, precisely,' said the Controller. 'Our ancestors were so stupid and short-sighted that when the first

reformers came along and offered to deliver them from those horrible emotions, they wouldn't have anything to do with them.'

As Robert Nozick has pointed out, if there were a machine that offered all desirable experiences on demand, it is not clear that we would want to use it. The basis of many gratifications is precisely the challenge required to obtain them, and short-cutting this removes their appeal. Thus, paradoxically, in order to have the possibility of deep gratification, we need to admit the possibility of failure and frustration into our lives. It is necessary to have the possibility of unhappiness for happiness to have any meaning.

At the end of *Brave new world*, the rebel John (aka the Savage) confronts the controller. Universal happiness, the controller admits, has been achieved by shifting the emphasis away from truth and beauty and towards comfort. Art and science have become impossible, because they require challenge, skill, and frustration. Happiness has got to be paid for somehow and the guarantee of comfort requires losing other experiences that are part of being human. Says the Savage:

'But I don't want comfort. I want God, I want poetry, I want real danger, I want freedom, I want goodness, I want sin.'

'In fact,' said Mustapha Mond, 'you're claiming the right to be unhappy.'

'All right, then,' said the Savage defiantly, 'I'm claiming the right to be unhappy.'

'Not to mention the right to grow old and ugly and impotent; the right to have syphilis and cancer; the right to have too little to eat; the right to be lousy; the right to live in constant apprehension of what may happen tomorrow; the right to catch typhoid; the right to be tortured by unspeakable pains of every kind.'

There was a long silence.

'I claim them all,' said the Savage at last.

In his dying hours, the Anglo-Austrian philosopher Ludwig Wittgenstein (1889–1951) is reported to have said to his landlady, 'Tell them I've had a wonderful life!' Wittgenstein's life had not been a happy one. He was a notoriously tortured, melancholic, irritable, and self-loathing man. He had published only one thing from his prodigious philosophical output during his lifetime, the *Tractatus logico-philosophicus*, and he had renounced that. Several times he had tried to give up philosophy altogether, becoming a harsh schoolteacher among other things. He saw his later (posthumously published) work partly as an attempt to release the mind from the grip of philosophical problems, which seem to have afflicted him almost like physical pains.

Wittgenstein's life was certainly a well-lived one, in terms of a level three conception which includes a wide range of human goods and the fulfilment of one's potential. It was certainly not a happy one, in a level one or two sense of positive emotion, or satisfaction with emotional experience. When Wittgenstein claimed that it had been wonderful, he was thus correct in one sense. He had made arguably the profoundest philosophical contribution of the twentieth century, probing deep into questions about logic, language, personal identity, culture, and the philosophy of mind. His influence, at first directly through his students, then indirectly through his readers, was to be extraordinary. In another sense, he had been in emotional agony a great deal of the time. Moreover, there is more than a sugges-tion that he was driven to achieve what he did at level three *because* he was so tortured at the emotional level.

The question is whether this is a price worth paying. In one sense, the answer is an obvious 'yes'. I would rather live in a world where Wittgenstein produced the *Philosophical investigations* than a world where he was happy. Of course, there is a self–other gap here. I am quite glad I am a reader of Wittgenstein rather than having to be Ludwig himself. But Wittgenstein is a very extreme example. There are plenty of other people whom I admire not for their happiness but for their dedication to some other human good or purpose. By pursuing their calling, they will expose themselves to frustration and the possibility of unhappiness. But, since total happiness is a mirage, this is a perfectly sensible thing to do. With important but limited returns from happiness, we may as well attempt to broaden our holding in the other stocks that make up good human life, such as purpose, community, solidarity, truth, justice, and beauty.

This conclusion echoes that of Positive Psychology, of numerous self-help books, and of many spiritual and social movements. Some caveats are in order, though. First, the sentiment expressed above can easily slip from being a piece of sensible advice to becoming a moral exhortation, and then it becomes problematic. Psychologists are welcome to self-actualize as much as they like, as long as they do it in the privacy of their own homes, but they should not diminish those who have different interests from themselves. Psychology research can demonstrate some general principles; that complete hedonic happiness is very hard to sustain, that the satisfaction of desires is subject to habituation, that a complex self is a buffer against depression, and so on, and these are useful facts to know. But ultimately people should be the arbiters of their own satisfaction, and certainly should not feel shame or guilt if their interests are not writing novels and exploring the Amazon. Being happy is no more reprehensible than it is essential.

The second point is that although psychology can suggest that experiencing flow or having a sense of purpose is an important component of well-being, it cannot, unfortunately, answer the question of what purpose one should have, or where one's flow will come from. That is an individual journey everyone has to make, and the answer will be different for everyone.

What of the future of happiness? Will human happiness be perfected as economic development continues? We have seen plenty of reasons why we should not expect this to happen. Average self-reported happiness is already fairly high, though below the maximum. The very design features of happiness—its use of social comparison, its tendency to return to a set point, its sources in so many mutually exclusive activities— militate against achieving any definitive resolution, whatever level of affluence is reached. As we have seen, average levels of happiness have shown no rise over the last half century, despite massive gains in material wealth.

So perhaps there is no prospect of happiness rising much more. But what of the opposite danger, happiness declining? It is an attractive myth to think that people were happier in the good old days, that somehow life was good simply because we were poorer, and such views are generally based on nostalgia rather than evidence. However, though the average level of happiness is fairly flat, there are some alarming trends amongst the most unhappy people. Rates of depression, for example, have risen very sharply in the developed economies in recent decades. This is a difficult issue to disentangle, since depression has always been quite prevalent, but in the past much of it was hidden or presented as some more socially acceptable physical symptom. People are becoming more open, and since treatments now have fewer side-effects, are more likely to medicalize their condition. However, the best controlled studies suggest that there is a genuine increase in distress, not just an increase in reporting. Other indicators point the same way. Suicides amongst young people have risen in recent decades, and though life expectancy is at its highest ever, in the USA at least, people rate their health as less good than they did in 1975.

What could account for this alarming trend? Although the opportunities for fulfilment are probably greater now than ever before, the pressures on our emotional psychology are also very intense. For one thing, global communications mean that we are exposed to a wider and wider range of material goods and social comparators. Our psychology of social status has evolved to handle living in a small band with a few dozen rivals in terms of intelligence, attractiveness, or status. Today, through books, magazines and television, we are exposed to the most beautiful, most talented, and most successful people from a global population of 6 billion. This means that whatever it is that we in particular do, there will be quite a few others to whom we are exposed who do it a lot better. No wonder there is so much anxiety about body shape, earning power, and career success.

Allied to the broadened scope of social comparison is the greater availability of material goods exquisitely designed to send our psychology of desire into over-drive. In the 1950s, it was seriously suggested, project-ing gains in productivity forward, that by the turn of the millennium we would be working about 16 hours a week. A new golden age of leisure was coming. The reality is rather different. People are working as hard as they ever have, resulting in massive increases in the amount of productive activity. The social scientists who foresaw the age of leisure failed to see that human motivation is driven by wanting rather than by liking. People who work part-time, control their own lives, join community organizations, or get involved in active leisure are happier than those who do not. Yet the vast majority of people do not make these choices. Instead, their positional psychology drives them to work harder and harder to amass a greatly increased range of material goods. All the evidence is that such goods do nothing to increase their happiness, but the urge to keep up with the Joneses is very strong. And as Robert Frank has argued, the vast amounts of money that go into conspicuous consumerism represent a huge diversion of resources that could be spent in other ways, if only the positional psychology could be overcome.

Related to individual consumption is the change in our patterns of social behaviour over recent decades. These changes have been exhaustively documented for the United States by social scientist Robert Puttnam. Since the end of the Second World War, geographical mobility and the average distance commuted to work have greatly increased. Meanwhile, membership of voluntary organizations, clubs, and community associations has steadily decreased. People have each other around to their homes less, and meet less often in local social contexts. In short, people spend more time working, travelling to work, and in their homes watching television, and less time doing everything else, from boy scouts to amateur music-making. Puttnam points out that the loss of this kind of informal activity is a loss to civic life because it creates what he calls social capital—an informal network of mutual aid and information exchange that keeps communities thriving.

From a psychological perspective, social capital is a potential buffer against stress and alienation, and so it is no wonder that its decline is associated with rises in depression. Most importantly, a community with high social capital is one in which the selves of the individuals within it are complex. This is because they are not just the local lawyer, but also the coach of the cricket team, the friendly neighbour, and the person who always sings at the christmas party. Thus they are better buffered against setbacks in their law job than a person who merely works, drives back from work to a place miles away, and then watches television. As the self simplifies, the circle of concern around the self narrows. Evidence of this comes from the annual survey that the University of California, Los Angeles does of its new students' values. In 1966, nearly 60% of incoming students rated it as essential or very important to keep up with politics, whilst in 1970, 30% felt it essential or very important to participate in community action. By 1995, fewer than 30% felt the same about politics, and around 20% about community action. Meanwhile, the percentage who felt it was essential or very important to be very well-off financially rose from only 44% in 1966 to 75% in 1998. We have already seen how materialism can breed discontent, and thus contemporary young people are putting an enormous amount of pressure on their narrow desires for material success.

The final reason that the dangers of chronic unhappiness are perhaps particularly acute at present is that our expectation of happiness has become so high. I believe that all cultures have a concept of happiness, and conceive of it as desirable. Happiness is more than just a social construction in that sense. However, in much poorer societies, or societies with a more collectivist ethos rather than the rampant individualism of the West, the constraints on individual action are such that the focus in seeking happiness is probably different. Given a context in which all one could do was labour in the fields or factories, one would have to focus on level one happiness (taking those moments of joy which came along), or level three goods (being as good a company man, father, neighbour, village elder as one could), since there was limited scope for individual action at level two. Rising affluence means that it is now possible to live in an almost infinite number of different ways and places pursuing an infinite number of different vocations and avocations. Such freedom is progress, but the choice can overwhelm with the possibility that the grass is greener somewhere else, and raise the expectation that complete happiness is out there to be had.

The self-help culture is not always beneficial in this way, since it can raise unrealistic expectations that everyone can find bliss and fulfilment all the time. Whilst its pronouncements are meant as inspiration, they can subtly convey the message that if someone is not totally level two happy this is probably their fault. They do not speak nearly enough of the fact that all paths have ups and downs, and all decisions involve trading off one benefit against another. As the circle of concern around the self has narrowed, expectations for the potential of subjective quality in personal experience have of course been raised. Whilst this must represent progress in human development, it is important to keep one's feet on the ground.

There is a considerable counter-culture developing against some of these trends. More and more people feel the need to downsize from the rat race, seek out functioning communities, or eschew consumerism in favour of voluntary simplicity. Certainly evidence shows that working part time or taking part in voluntary and community activities has real benefits in terms of personal well-being. As yet society is not well set up to accommodate such arrangements, but one can only predict that the demand for them will grow. As Robert

Frank has argued, because of the positional psychology of work and consumption, if we could all agree to take downsizing steps simultaneously, then no-one would actually lose relative position. This would of course be hard to implement, and so for now, it may continue to be a question of most of the population living a life driven by wanting whilst a few attempt to carve out a niche based on liking.

We end this brief investigation of happiness, then, with the notion that it is not in fact the only or ultimate good. There is, of course, the negative–positive asymmetry. If you are actively unhappy, you need to do something about it because the potent negative emotions invade our health and hamper our ability to concentrate on other things. But if you are above neutral, but below the maximum most of the time, then this is probably as good as it gets. This is perhaps hard to swallow in a culture that has become obsessed with personal feeling. But paradoxically, shifting attention to those broader themes can be worthwhile not just in its own right, but because it reduces dissatisfaction in the hedonic domain too. Sometimes it may be better to get a little out of touch with your feelings, and try to concentrate on other things that you see as worthwhile or challenging or important. The broader your investment in human goods, the more your portfolio is buffered, and the more variegated life can be. And here is the last twist in the happiness tale. If you do this, you might just notice one day that happiness has arrived unannounced. As Nathaniel Hawthorne put it:

> Happiness is a butterfly, which, when pursued, is always beyond our grasp, but which, if you will sit down quietly, may alight upon you.

Further reading

Research studies in the field of hedonics are generally not technically difficult to read, and so the reader wishing to go deeper into the scientific basis of this book is encouraged to consult the original sources listed in the References section. The most useful single book source is Daniel Kahneman, Ed Diener and Norbert Schwarz (eds), *Well-being: The foundations of hedonic psychology* (New York: Russell Sage Foundation 1999). This is a seminal overview of the field, with contributions from almost all of the leading players. Accessible but older overviews are David Lykken's *Happiness* (New York: Golden Books 1999) and Michael Argyle's *The psychology of happiness* (London: Routledge 1987).

For readers wanting to investigate the emotions in general a little further, try Dylan Evans' *Emotion: The science of sentiment* (Oxford: Oxford University Press 2001). For information on depression and emotional disorders, Peter Whybrow's *A mood apart: A thinker's guide to emotion and its disorders* (New York: Basic Books 1997) is excellent. Robert Sapolsky summarizes research on stress, and the interactions between mind and body, in *Why zebras don't get ulcers: An updated guide to stress, stress-related diseases, and coping* (New York: W.H. Freeman 1998). On mental health and distress in general, and treatments, Raj Persaud's *Staying sane: How to make your mind work for you* (Revised edition, London: Bantam Books 2001) is very good. More practical advice on overcoming depression is given by Paul Gilbert in *Overcoming depression* (Revised edition, London: Constable and Robinson 2000).

The landmark volume in the paradigm of positive psychology is Martin Seligman's *Authentic happiness* (New York: The Free Press 2002). Milhayi Csikszentmihalyi's work on the quality of experience and the good life is laid out in his *Flow: The psychology of optimal experience* (New York: Harper and Row 1990) and *Living well: The psychology of everyday life* (New York: Basic Books 1997). For a well-written exploration of some of the paradoxes and tensions in the pursuit of happiness, try Ziyad Marar's *The happiness paradox* (London: Reaktion Books 2003). More philosophical explorations of happiness, consolation, and the good life are undertaken by Alain de Botton in *The consolations of philosophy* (London: Hamish Hamilton 2000) and *Status anxiety* (London: Hamish Hamilton 2004). Finally, for an excellent development of the thesis that we have inherited a set of relatively automatic psychological mechanisms for following evolution's purposes rather than our own, and also relatively flexible, rational higher cognitive processes that we can use to defuse these inbuilt urges, see Keith Stanovich's *The robot's rebellion: Finding meaning in the age of Darwin* (Chicago: University of Chicago Press 2004).

Many of the most stimulating contributions to the debates about the sources of human happiness come from outside psychology. From economics, there is Robert Frank's *Luxury fever: Why money fails to satisfy in an era of excess* (New York: The Free Press 1999), and from evolutionary biology, Terry Burnham and Jay Phelan's *Mean genes: Can we tame our primal instincts?* (London: Simon and Schuster 2000). Robert Puttnam's groundbreaking work on the decline, and beneficial effects, of social capital is laid out in his *Bowling alone: The collapse and revival of American community* (New York: Simon and Schuster 2000).

Notes

20 *Eudaimonia* as distinct from subjective happiness: Kraut 1979; Ryff 1989.

21 Bentham and the classical economists: Bentham 1789.

24 Carol Ryff's research on psychological well-being: Ryff 1989; Ryff and Keyes 1995; Keyes, Shmotkin and Ryff 2002. Quote from Ryff and Keyes 1995, page 725.

25.1 Positive Psychology: Seligman 2002.

25.2 Flow: Csikszentmihalyi 1990.

26 The autotelic personality: Csikszentmilhalyi 1997, quote from page 114.

27.1 Studies of musicians, writers and artists: Jamison 1989; Post 1994; Ludwig 1995; Nettle 2001.

27.2 Very happy people: Diener and Seligman 2002.

27.3 Life with flow more worth living: Csikszentmilhalyi 1997, page 113.

28 Seligman's definition of happiness: Seligman 2002, page 261.

29 The valid point that Ryff, Seligman and Csikszentmilhalyi all make: This is a simplification, and there are further philosophical issues here which cannot be gone into in detail. If there are many other human goods which are distinct from happiness but nonetheless worth pursuing, what makes them good? An immediate response would be that they are good because they increase happiness (our own or someone else's). But then they *would* be reducible to happiness after all. The issue is that happiness is one of the few things that is self-justifying, whereas other important goods like justice, beauty, purpose, and community are easiest to justify (for the non-religious) by appealing to happiness. One possible solution to the paradox is to say

that there are other goods that are distinct from *immediate* happiness, though they might be related to future or indirect happiness.

30 *Authentic happiness* vs. *The good life:* Csikszentmilhalyi titled an earlier book *Living well* (Csikszentmilhalyi 1997), and this is perhaps a better catchphrase for the positive psychology enterprise than *Authentic happiness.*

33 Sources of joy: Scherer, Summerfield and Wallbott 1983; Argyle 1987, Chapter 7.

34 Dime on the photocopier: Schwarz and Strack 1999.

35.1 Effects of context on judgements of happiness: Schwartz and Strack 1999.

35.2 Weather and life satisfaction study: Schwartz and Clore 1983.

36.1 Happiness as the balance of pleasure and pain: The view can be traced back at least to John Stuart Mill. See Parducci 1995.

36.2 Independence of positive and negative emotions: Diener and Emmons 1985.

36.3 Some people have more ups and downs than others: Larsen and Diener 1987.

37 Remembering life events affects life satisfaction: Strack, Schwarz and Gschniedinger 1985.

38.1 Photographs of models and mate satisfaction: Kenrick, Gutierres and Goldberg 1989.

38.2 Bronze and silver Olympic medallists: Medvec, Madey and Gilovich 1985.

38.3 Mencken: Quoted in Frank 1999.

39.1 Overestimation of impact of life events on happiness: Loewenstein and Schkade 1999.

39.2 Lottery winners: Brickman, Coates and Janoff-Bulman 1978.

40   Mugs and the endowment effect: Kahneman, Knetsch and Thaler 1991.

41   Hands in cold water study: Kahneman, Frederickson, Schreiber and Redelmeier 1993.

42   Subjective versus objective happiness, and the peak-end rule: Kahneman 1999.

Chapter 2

45   Schopenhauer on suffering: Schopenhauer 1851/1970.

46   Juvenal on bread and circuses: *Satire X*, Ramsay 1918.

47   Match quotations to photographs: 1. Freud, 2. Sartre, 3. Nietzsche, 4. Wittgenstein, 5. Schopenhauer, 6. Larkin.

48   The NCDS: The data are accessible through *http://www.data-archive.ac.uk*. Information on the study is available from *http://www.cls.ioe.ac.uk/Cohort/Ncds/mainncds.htm*

49.1 Most people are happy: Diener and Diener 1996.

49.2 Cross-national surveys: Diener and Suh 1999.

51   Table 2.1: Data from Diener and Suh 1999.

52.1 Geoffrey Miller: Miller 2000.

52.2 Adam Smith: Smith 1759.

53.1 Higher levels of happiness reported face-to-face than by post: Smith 1979. Experimenters of the opposite sex: Strack, Schwarz, Kern and Wagner 1990.

53.2 People describe themselves as better than average: Alicke 1985; Svenson 1981; Weinstein 1980.

54   Self-enhancement as a response to uncertainty: Taylor and Brown 1988; Nettle 2004a.

60   Margaret Mead and Samoa: Mead 1929; Freeman 1983.

Chapter 3

65.1 The origins of this famous dictum turn out to be obscure. Erik Eriksen attributed it to Freud, but it is apparently not to be found in his written works. See *http://www.freud.org.uk/fmfaq.htm*

65.2 Transformation of hysteric misery into common unhappiness: Freud and Breuer 1894/2004.

65.3 Asking a bald person for advice on your hairstyle: A Hausa proverb in fact. Roughly, *A tambaya mai kundumi labarin kitso.*

66 Consistency and validity of self-reported happiness: Diener 1994; Diener, Diener and Diener 1995; Sandvik, Diener and Siedlitz 1993.

67 Study of positive emotion and longevity in nuns: Danner, Snowden and Friesen 2001.

69 Women's greater emotionality: Nolen-Hoeksma and Rusting 1999.

70 Low life satisfaction among the unemployed: Tiggeman and Winefield 1984.

72 Well being fails to increase as incomes grow: Myers and Diener 1996.

73 Importance of relative rather than absolute wealth for life satisfaction: Frank 1999.

75.1 Studies of British civil servants: Bosma *et al.* 1997; Marmot *et al.* 1997; Marmot 2003.

75.2 The idea of adaptation: Brickman and Campbell 1971; Brickman, Coates and Janoff-Bulman 1978.

76 Easterlin's study of the hedonic treadmill: Easterlin 2003.

78 Explaining national differences in well-being: Diener and Suh 1999.

80 Marriage and life satisfaction: Haring-Hidore, Stock, Okun and Witter 1985.

81.1 Personality factors affect patterns of marriage and divorce: Kelly and Conley 1987; Nettle in press.

81.2 German study of marriage and life satisfaction: Lucas, Clark, Georgellis and Diener 2003.

83 Disabilities and health problems affect life happiness: Brickman, Coates and Janoff-Bulman 1978; Schulz and Dekker 1995.

84.1 Failure to adapt to noise: Weinstein 1982.

84.2 Cosmetic surgery and satisfaction: Klassen, Jenkinson, Fitzpatrick and Goodacre 1996.

85.1 A set point of happiness to which we return: Lykken and Tellegen 1996.

85.2 Frank on positional and non-positional goods: Frank 1999.

Chapter 4

92.1 Studies on the temporal stability of happiness: Diener and Larsen 1984; Costa, McCrae and Zonderman 1987; Diener *et al.* 1993.

92.2 Some people get more enjoyment across situations: Diener and Larsen 1984.

93 Happiness in identical twins: Tellegen and Lykken 1996.

97.1 Habits of extroverts: Furnham and Heaven 1999. Sexual behaviour of extroverts: Nettle in press.

97.2 Incentive salience explanation of extroversion: Depue and Collins 1999.

99 Online psychology laboratory:
http://www.psychresearch.org.uk. Please log on and take part in future studies!

101.1 Neuroticism inversely correlated with happiness: Costa and McCrae 1980; Hayes and Joseph 2003.

101.2 Neuroticism associated with creativity and achievement: Jamison 1989; Feist 1999; Nettle 2001 and references therein; Nowakowska *et al.* in press.

102   Extroversion positively correlated with happiness: Costa and McCrae 1980; Hayes and Joseph 2003.

104.1 Personalities of very happy people: Diener and Seligman 2002.

104.2 Drawbacks of extroversion: Nettle in press; Joinson and Nettle submitted.

104.3 Personality traits other than extroversion and neuroticism: Hayes and Joseph 2003.

106   Australian study of personality and life events: Headey and Wearing 1983.

107   Further studies of personality and life events: Magnus *et al.* 1993.

111   Table 4.1: The table has been compiled from several sources using slightly different statistics and methodology, and as such the figures are estimates only. Most importantly, the diversity of the sample is different in different cases so the variation will be apportioned differently across factors. Social class is not identical to income as it is based on a classification of occupations in terms of professional standing rather than financial reward. The sources used are: Sex: Haring, Stock and Okun 1984; Age: Argyle 1999; Social Class and Income: Haring, Stock and Okun 1984; Marital status: NCDS data; Neuroticism and Extroversion: Costa and McCrae 1980; Hills and Argyle 2001; Nettle, unpublished data

from online survey; Other personality factors: Nettle, unpublished data from online survey; Hayes and Joseph 2003.

112 Lykken and Tellegen quote: Lykken and Tellegen 1996, p. 189.

114 Seeking broader goods than just level two happiness: Seligman 2002.

Chapter 5

116.1 Prozac and the better-than-well phenomenon: Kramer 1993.

116.2 SSRI increases positive emotionality in healthy volunteers: Knutson *et al.* 1998.

117 SSRI prescription levels and trends: McManus *et al.* 2000.

118 Key study of the effect of d-fenfluramine: Meyer *et al.* 2003.

119 Treating a low serotonin society: James 1998.

120.1 Brain activity of cocaine addicts: Grant *et al.* 1996.

120.2 Hyperactive amygdala in depression: Kennedy, Javanmard and Vaccarino 1997.

120.3 Effects of amygdala damage in humans: Adolphs, Tranel, Damasio and Damasio 1995.

120.4 Activity in monkey amygdala and nucleus accumbens anticipates reward: Schulz, Dayan and Montague 1997; Hoebel *et al.* 1999.

122.1 Brain activity of males looking at female faces: Aharon *et al.* 2001.

122.2 Brain stimulation reward: Shizgal 1999.

125.1 Transcranial magnetic stimulation: Gershon, Darnon and Grunhaus 2003.

125.2 Rats work to self-inject dopamine: Hoebel *et al.* 1983.

125.3 Wanting and liking separable in rats: Berridge and Valenstein 1991; Berridge 1999.

127.1 Opiates enhance eating pleasure in rats: Peciña and Berridge 1995.

127.2 Opiates affect pleasure from food in humans: Drewnowski *et al.* 1995.

128 Study of heroin addicts: Lamb *et al.* 1991.

130 Low serotonin activity in depression and suicidality: Meyer *et al.* 2003. Low serotonin activity in violent men: Moffitt *et al.* 1998.

131.1 Serotonin influencing drugs increasing co-operation and sociability: Tse and Bond 2002; Knutson *et al.* 1998.

131.2 Stress hormones and serotonin related to rank in monkeys. Ralcigh *et al.* 1984, 1991; Sapolsky 1998. Rather confusingly, administration of an SSRI to a small American lizard, the Green Anole, has precisely the opposite effect, causing dominant individuals to lose status (Larson and Summers 2001). It may be that in lizards, status is maintained by aggression, whereas in primates it is maintained by alliances. SSRI administration would reduce the former and facilitate the latter.

132.1 The stress system: Sapolsky 1998.

132.2 Studies of new and insecure employees: Kramer 1994.

133 Debate about nature and function of depression: Nesse 2000; Watson and Andrews 2003; Nettle 2004b.

134 History of MDMA/Ecstasy: Rosenbaum 2002. Negative effects of Ecstasy: McCardle *et al.* 2004; Curran *et al.* 2004.

136.1 Brain activity in amusement, sadness and depression: Davidson *et al.* 1990; Lévesque *et al.* 2003; Pizzagalli *et al.* 2002.

136.2 Asymmetry of cerebral activity and emotional response to film clips: Wheeler, Davidson and Tomarken 1993.

137 Rosenkrantz study of cerebral activity and immune response: Rosenkrantz *et al.* 2003.

138.1 Stress system and its pathological engagement: Sapolsky 1998.

138.2 Emotional style and brain activity asymmetry in children: Davidson and Fox 1989.

140 Genes and personality dimensions: Lesch *et al.* 1996; Ebstein *et al.* 1996; Munafo *et al.* 2003.

Chapter 6

142 Self-help titles: Norcross 2000.

145 Effectiveness of self-help books: McKendree-Smith, Floyd and Scogin 2003. Happiness training programmes: Fordyce 1977, 1983, Fava and Ruini 2003.

148 Cognitive behavourial therapy: Beck 1967.

149 Natural selection doesn't give a fig for our happiness: Nesse 1999, page 433.

150.1 Effectiveness of CBT: Miller and Berman 1983.

150.2 CBT affects brain activity: Goldapple *et al.* 2004.

151 Pleasant activities training: Fordyce 1977, 1983; Turner, Ward and Turner 1979.

152 The more important people believe finanical success to be, the less their satisfaction: Nickerson *et al.* 2003.

153 Overestimating the impact of life events on happiness: Loewenstein and Schkade 1999.

154   The negative emotion system is supposed to be hyperactive: Nesse 2001.

155   John Stuart Mill and the paradox of hedonism: Mill 1909.

156.1   Faith, health and happiness: Myers, 2000; Powell, Shahabi and Thoresen 2003; Seeman, Dublin and Seeman 2003.

156.2   Linville's work on self-concept: Linville 1985, 1987.

157.1   Effect of voluntary work and community organizations on happiness: Puttnam 2000.

157.2   Beneficial effects of meditation: Leung and Singhal 2004; Davidson *et al.* 2003.

158.1   Mindfulness-based cognitive therapy: Segal, Williams and Teasdale 2001.

158.2   Beneficial effects of writing: Pennebaker 1997; Burton and King 2004.

159   William James quotation: James 1890, cited in De Botton 2004, page 56.

160   John Keats, *Epistle to J.H. Reynolds.*

Chapter 7

161   Arthur Miller: Quoted in Marar 2003, page 173.

172   Robert Nozick: Nozick 1974.

173   Wittgenstein's life: Monk 1990.

177.1   Rising rates of depression: Klerman *et al.* 1985; Murphy 1986; Lewis *et al.* 1993.

177.2   Decline in self-rated health in the USA: Puttnam 2000, page 332.

184   Nathaniel Hawthorne: Quoted in Marar 2003, page 28.

References

Adolphs, R., Tranel, D., Damasio, H. and Damasio, A.R. (1995). Fear and the human amygdala. *Journal of Neuroscience*, **15**, 5879–91.

Aharon, I. et al. (2001). Beautiful faces have variable reward value: fMRI and behavioural evidence. *Neuron*, **32**, 537–51.

Alicke, M.D. (1985). Global self-evaluation as defined by the desirability and controllability of trait adjectives. *Journal of Personality and Social Psychology*, **49**, 1621–30.

Argyle, M. (1987). *The psychology of happiness*. Routledge, London.

Argyle, M. (1999). Causes and correlates of happiness. In Kahneman, Diener and Schwarz (1999), pp. 354–73.

Barkow, J. Cosmides, L. and Tooby, J. (eds). (1992). *The adapted mind: Evolutionary psychology and the generation of culture*. Oxford University Press, New York.

Beck, A.T. (1976). *Cognitive therapy and the emotional disorders*. International Universities Press, New York.

Bentham, J. (1789). *An enquiry into the principle of morals and legislation*. London.

Berridge, K. (1999). Pleasure, pain, desire and dread: Hidden core processes of emotion. In Kahneman, Diener and Schwarz (1999), pp. 525–57.

Berridge, K. and Valenstein, E.S. (1991). What psychological process mediates feeding evoked by electrical stimulation of the lateral hypothalamus? *Behavioral Neuroscience*, **103**, 36–45.

Bosma, H. et al. (1997). Low job control and risk of coronary heart disease in the Whitehall II (prospective cohort) study. *British Medical Journal*, **314**, 558–65.

Brickman, P. and Campbell, D.T. (1971). Hedonic relativism and planning the good society. In M.H. Appley (ed.), *Adaptation level theory*, pp. 287–305. Academic Press, New York.

Brickman, P., Coates, D. and Janoff-Bulman, R. (1978). Lottery winners and accident victims: Is happiness relative? *Journal of Personality and Social Psychology*, **36**, 917–27.

Burton, C.M. and King, L.A. (2004). Health benefits of writing about intensely positive experiences. *Journal of Research in Personality*, **38**, 150–63.

Buss, D. (1999). *Evolutionary psychology*. Allyn & Bacon, London.

Cosmides, L. and Tooby, J. (1987). From evolution to behaviour: Evolutionary psychology as the missing link. In J. Dupre (ed.), *The latest on the best: Essays on evolution and optimality*. MIT Press, Cambridge, MA.

Costa, P.T. and McRae, R.R. (1980). Influence of extraversion and neuroticism on subjective well-being: Happy and unhappy people. *Journal of Personality and Social Psychology*, **38**, 668–78.

Costa, P.T., McRae, R.R. and Zonderman, A. (1987). Environmental and dispositional influences on well-being: Longitudinal follow-up of an American national sample. *British Journal of Psychology*, **78**, 299–306.

Csikszentmihalyi, M. (1990). *Flow: The psychology of optimal experience*. Harper and Row, New York.

Csikszentmihalyi, M. (1997). *Living well: The psychology of everyday life*. Weidenfeld and Nicholson, London.

Curran, H., Rees, H., Hoare, T., Hoshi, R. and Bond, A. (2004). Empathy and aggression: two faces of ecstasy? A study of interpretative cognitive bias and mood change in ecstasy users. *Psychopharmacology*, **173**, 425–33.

Dalai Lama, and Cutler, H. (1998). *The art of happiness*. Hodder & Stoughton, London.

Danner, D., Snowdon, D. and Friesen, W. (2001). Positive emotions in early life and longevity: Findings from the Nun study. *Journal of Personality and Social Psychology*, **80**, 804–13.

Davidson, R.J. and Fox, N.A. (1989). Frontal brain asymmetry predicts infants' response to maternal separation. *Journal of Abnormal Psychology*, **98**, 127–31.

Davidson, R.J. et al. (1990). Approach-withdrawal and cerebral asymmetry: I. Emotional expression and brain physiology. *Journal of Personality and Social Psychology*, **58**, 330–41.

Davidson, R.J. et al. (2003). Alterations in brain and immune function produced by mindfulness meditation. *Psychosomatic Medicine*, **65**, 564–70.

De Botton, A. (2004). *Status anxiety*. Penguin, London.

Depue, R.A. and Collins, P.F. (1999). Neurobiology of the structure of personality: Dopamine, facilitation of incentive motivation, and extraversion. *Behavioral and Brain Sciences*, **22**, 491–520.

Diener, E. (1994). Assessing subjective well-being: Progress and opportunities. *Social Indicators Research*, **31**, 103–57.

Diener, E. and Diener, C. (1996). Most people are happy. *Psychological Science*, **7**, 181–5.

Diener, E., Diener, M. and Diener, C. (1995). Factors predicting the subjective well-being of nations. *Journal of Personality and Social Psychology*, **69**, 851–64.

Diener, E. and Emmons, R.A. (1985). The independence of

positive and negative affect. *Journal of Personality and Social Psychology*, **50**, 1031–8.

Diener, E. and Larsen, R.J. (1984). Temporal stability and cross-situational consistency of affective, behavioral and cognitive responses. *Journal of Personality and Social Psychology*, **66**, 1128–39.

Diener, E., Sandvik, E., Pavot, W. and Diener, M. (1993). The relationship between income and subjective well-being: Relative or absolute? *Social Indicators Research*, **28**, 195–213.

Diener, E. and Seligman, M.E.P. (2002). Very happy people. *Psychological Science*, **13**, 81–4.

Diener, E. and Suh, E. M. (1999). National differences in subjective well-being. In Kahneman, Diener and Schwarz (1999), pp. 434–52.

Drenowski, A. et al. (1995). Naloxone, an opiate blocker, reduces the consumption of sweet high-fat foods in obese and lean female binge eaters. *American Journal of Clinical Nutrition*, **61**, 1206–2.

Easterlin, R.A. (2003). Explaining happiness. *Proceedings of the National Academy of Sciences*, **100**, 11176–83.

Ebstein, R. et al. (1996). Dopamine D4 receptor Exon III polymorphism associated with the human personality trait of sensation-seeking. *Nature Genetics*, **12**, 78–80.

Ekman, P. (1992). An argument for basic emotions. *Cognition and Emotion*, **6**, 169–200.

Evans, D. (2001). *Emotion*. Oxford University Press, Oxford.

Fava, G. and Ruini, C. (2003). Development and characteristics of a well-being enhancing psychotherapeutic strategy: well-being therapy. *Journal of Behavior Therapy and Experimental Psychiatry*, **34**, 45–63.

Feist, G.J. (1999). The influence of personality on artistic and scientific creativity. In R.J. Sternberg (ed.), *Handbook of creativity*, pp. 273–95. Cambridge University Press, Cambridge.

Fordyce, M.W. (1977). Development of a program to increase personal happiness. *Journal of Counseling Psychology*, **24**, 511–21.

Fordyce, M.W. (1983). A program to increase happiness: Further studies. *Journal of Counseling Psychology*, **30**, 483–98.

Frank, R.H. (1999). *Luxury fever: Why money fails to satisfy in an era of excess*. The Free Press, New York.

Freeman, D. (1983). *Margaret Mead and Samoa: The making and unmaking of an anthropological myth*. Harvard University Press, Cambridge, MA.

Freud, S. and Breuer, J. (1994/2004). *Studies in hysteria*. Penguin Modern Classics, London.

Furnham, A. and Heaven, P. (1999). *Personality and social behaviour*. Arnold, London.

Gershon, A.A., Darnon, P.N. and Grunhaus, L. (2003). Transcranial magnetic stimulation in the treatment of depression. *American Journal of Psychiatry*, **160**, 835–45.

Goldapple, K. et al. (2004). Modulation of cortical-limbic pathways in major depression—treatment-specific effects of cognitive behavior therapy. *Archives of General Psychiatry*, **61**, 34–41.

Grant, S. et al. (1996). Activation of memory circuits during cue-elicited cocaine craving. *Proceedings of the National Academy of Sciences of the USA*, **93**, 12040–5.

Haring, M., Stock, W.A. and Okun, M.A. (1984). A research synthesis of gender and social class as correlates of subjective well-being. *Human Relations*, **37**, 645–57.

Haring-Hidore, M., Stock, W. A., Okun, M. A. and Witter, R. A. (1985). Marital status and subjective well-being: A research synthesis. *Journal of Marriage and the Family*, **47**, 947–53.

Hayes, N. and Joseph, S. (2003). Big five correlates of three measures of subjective well-being. *Personality and Individual Differences*, **34**, 723–7.

Headey, B. and Wearing, A. (1989). Personality, life events and subjective well-being: Toward a dynamic equilibrium model. *Journal of Personality and Social Psychology*, **57**, 731–9.

Heidenreich, T. and Michalak, J. (2003). Mindfulness as a treatment principle in behaviour therapy. *Verhaltenstherapie*, **13**, 264–74.

Hills, P. and Argyle, M. (2001). Emotional stability as a major dimension of happiness. *Personality and Individual Differences*, **31**, 1357–64.

Hoebel, B.G. et al. (1983). Self-administration of dopamine directly into the brain. *Psychopharmacology*, **81**, 158–63.

Hoebel, B.G., Rada, P.V., Mark, G.P. and Pothos, E.N. (1999). Neural systems for reinforcement and inhibition of behavior: Relevance to eating, addiction and depression. In Kahneman, Diener and Schwarz (1999), pp. 558–72.

James, O. (1998). *Britain on the couch: Treating a low serotonin society*. Arrow, London.

James, W. (1890). *Principles of psychology*. Henry Holt, New York.

Jamison, K.R. (1989). Mood disorders and patterns of creativity in British writers and artists. *Psychiatry*, **32**, 125–34.

Joinson, C. and Nettle D. (submitted). Sensation seeking in evolutionary context: Behaviour and life outcomes in a contemporary population. *Journal of Personality*.

Kahneman, D. (1999). Objective happiness. In Kahneman, Diener and Schwarz (1999), pp. 3–25.

Kahneman, D., Diener, E. and N. Schwarz (eds). (1999). *Wellbeing: Foundations of hedonic psychology.* Russell Sage Foundation, New York.

Kahneman, D., Frederickson, B.L., Schreiber, C.A. and Redelmeier, D.A. (1993). When more pain is preferred to less: Adding a better end. *Psychological Science,* 4, 401–5.

Kahneman, D., Knetsch, J.L. and Thaler, R.H. (1991). The endowment effect, loss aversion, and the status quo. *Journal of Economic Perspectives,* 5, 193–206.

Kahneman, D., Wakker, P. and Sarin, R. (1997). Back to Bentham? Explorations of experienced utility. *Quarterly Journal of Economics,* 112, 375–405.

Kennedy, M.F., Javanmard, M. and Vaccarino, F.J. (1997). A review of functional neuroimaging in mood disorders: Positron Emission Tomography and depression. *Canadian Journal of Psychiatry,* 42, 467–75.

Kenrick, D.T., Gutierres, S.E and Golberg, L.L. (1989). Influence of popular erotica on judgements of strangers and mates. *Journal of Experimental Social Psychology,* 25, 159–67.

Klassen, A., Jenkinson, C., Fitzpatrick, R. and Goodacre, T. (1996). Patients' health-related quality of life before and after aesthetic surgery. *British Journal of Plastic Surgery,* 49, 433–8.

Klerman, G.L. et al. (1985). Birth-cohort trends in rates of major depressive disorder among relatives of patients with affective disorder. *Archives of General Psychiatry,* 32, 689–95.

Knutson, B et al. (1998). Selective alteration of personality and social behaviour by serotonergic intervention. *American Journal of Psychiatry,* 15, 373–9.

Kramer, P. (1993). *Listening to Prozac*. Viking Penguin, New York.

Kramer, R.M. (1994). The sinister attribution error: Paranoid cognition and collective distrust in organizations. *Motivation and Emotion*, **18**, 199–230.

Kraut, R. (1979). Two conceptions of happiness. *Philosophical Review*, **88**, 167–97.

Lamb, R.J. et al. (1991). The reinforcing and subjective effects of morphine in post-addicts: A dose-response study. *Journal of Pharmacology and Experimental Therapies*, **259**, 1165–73.

Larsen, R.J. and Diener, E. (1987). Affect intensity as an individual difference characteristic: A review. *Journal of Research in Personality*, **21**, 1–39.

Larson, E.T. and Summers, C.H. (2001). Serotonin reverses dominant social status. *Behavioural Brain Research*, **121**, 95–102.

Lesch, K-P. et al. (1996). Association of anxiety-related traits with a polymorphism in the serotonin transporter gene regulatory region. *Science*, **274**, 1527–31.

Leung, Y. and Singhal, A. (2004). An examination of the relationship between Qigong relationship and personality. *Social Behavior and Personality*, **32**, 313–20.

Lévesque, J. et al. (2003). Neural correlates of feeling sad in healthy girls. *Neuroscience*, **121**, 545–51.

Lewis, G. et al. (1993). Another British disease? A recent increase in the prevalence of psychiatric morbidity. *Journal of Epidemiology and Community Health*, **47**, 358–61.

Linville, P.W. (1985). Self-complexity and affective extremity: Don't put all your eggs in one basket. *Social Cognition*, **3**, 94–120.

Linville, P.W. (1987). Self-complexity as a cognitive buffer against stress-related illness and depression. *Journal of Personality and Social Psychology*, **52**, 663–76.

Loewenstein, G. and Schkade, D. (1999). Wouldn't it be nice? Predicting future feelings. In Kahneman, Diener and Schwarz (1999), pp. 85–108.

Ludwig, A. (1995). *The price of greatness: Resolving the mad genius controversy*. Guilford Press, New York.

Lykken, D. and Tellegen, A. (1996). Happiness is a stochastic phenomenon. *Psychological Science*, **7**, 186–9.

McCardle, K., Luebbers, S., Carter, J.D., Croft, R.J. and Stough, C. (2004). Chronic MDMA (Ecstasy) use: Effects on cognition and mood. *Psychopharmacology*, **173**, 434–9.

McKendree-Smith, N.L., Floyd, M. and Scogin, F.R. (2003). Self-administered treatments for depression: A review. *Journal of Clinical Psychology*, **59**, 275–88.

McManus, P. et al. (2000). Recent trends in the use of anti-depressant drugs in Australia. *Medical Journal of Australia*, **173**, 458–61.

Magnus, K., Diener, E., Fujita, F. and Pavot, W. (1993). Extraversion and neuroticism as predictors of objective life events: A longitudinal analysis. *Journal of Personality and Social Psychology*, **65**, 1046–53.

Marar, Z. (2003). *The happiness paradox*. Reaktion Books, London.

Marmot, M.G. (2003). Understanding social inequalities in health. *Perspectives in Biology and Medicine*, **46**, S9–S23.

Marmot, M.G. et al.(1997). Contribution of job control and other risk factors to social variations in coronary heart disease. *Lancet*, **350**, 235–40.

Mead, M. (1929). *Coming of age in Samoa*. Jonathan Cape, London.

Medvec, V. H., Madey, S. F. and Gilovich, T. (1995). When less is more: Counterfactual thinking and satisfaction among Olympic medalists. *Journal of Personality and Social Psychology*, **69**, 603–10.

Meyer, J.H. et al. (2003). Dysfunctional attitudes and 5-HT$_2$ receptors during depression and self-harm. *American Journal of Psychiatry*, **160**, 90–9.

Mill, J.S. (1909). *Autobiography*. The Harvard Classics, volume 25. Collier and Company, New York.

Miller, G. F. (2000). *The mating mind*. Heinemann, London.

Miller, R.C. and Berman, J.S. (1983). The efficacy of cognitive behavior therapies: A quantitative review of the research evidence. *Psychological Bulletin*, **94**, 39–53.

Moffitt, T.E. et al. (1998). Whole blood serotonin relates to violence in an epidemiological study. *Biological Psychiatry*, **43**, 446–57.

Monk, R. (1990). *Ludwig Wittgenstein: The duty of genius*. Jonathan Cape, London.

Munafò, M.R. et al. (2003). Genetic polymorphisms and personality in healthy adults: A systematic review and meta-analysis. *Molecular Psychiatry*, **8**, 471–84.

Murphy, J.M. (1986). Trends in depression and anxiety: Men and women. *Acta Psychiatrica Scandinavica*, **73**, 113–27.

Myers, D.G. (2002). The funds, friends and faith of happy people. *American Psychologist*, **55**, 56–67.

Myers, D.G., and Diener, E. (1996). The pursuit of happiness. *Scientific American, May 1996*, 54–6.

Nesse, R.M. (1999). The evolution of hope and despair. *Social Research*, **66**, 429–69.

Nesse, R.M. (2000). Is depression an adaptation? *Archives of General Psychiatry*, **57**, 14–20.

Nesse, R.M. (2001). The smoke detector principle: Natural selection and the regulation of defenses. *Annals of the New York Academy of Sciences*, **935**, 75–85.

Nettle, D. (2001). *Strong imagination: Madness, creativity and human nature*. Oxford University Press, Oxford.

Nettle, D. (2004a). Adaptive illusions: Optimism, control and human rationality. In D. Evans and P. Cruse (eds), *Emotion, evolution and rationality*, pp. 191–206. Oxford University Press, Oxford.

Nettle, D. (2004b). Evolutionary origins of depression: A review and reformulation. *Journal of Affective Disorders*, **81**, 91–102.

Nettle, D. (in press). Personality as life history strategy: An evolutionary approach to the extraversion continuum. *Evolution and Human Behavior*.

Nickerson, C. et al. (2003). Zeroing in on the dark side of the American dream: A closer look at the negative consequences of the goal for financial success. *Psychological Science*, **14**, 531–6.

Nolen-Hoeksma, S. and Rusting, C. L. (1999). Gender differences in well-being. In Kahneman, Diener and Schwarz (1999), pp. 330–51.

Norcross, J.C. (2000). Here comes the self-help revolution in mental health. *Psychotherapy*, **37**, 370–7.

Nowakowska, C. et al. (in press). Temperamental commonalities and differences in euthymic mood disorder patients, creative controls, and healthy controls. *Journal of Affective Disorders*.

Nozick, R. (1974). *Anarchy, State and Utopia*. Basic Books, New York.

Parducci, A. (1995). *Happiness, pleasure and judgement: The contextual theory and its applications*. Erlbaum, Hillsdale, N.J.

Peciña, S., and Berridge, K. (1995). Central enhancement of

taste pleasure by intra-ventricular morphine. *Neurobiology*, **3**, 269–80.

Pennebaker, J.W. (1997). Writing about emotional experiences as a therapeutic process. *Psychological Science*, **8**, 162–6.

Pizzagalli, D.A. et al. (2002). Brain electrical tomography in depression: The importance of symptom severity, anxiety and melancholic features. *Biological Psychiatry*, **52**, 73–85.

Post, F. (1994). Creativity and psychopathology: A study of 291 word-famous men. *British Journal of Psychiatry*, **165**, 22–34.

Powell, L.H., Shahabi, S. and Thoresen, C.E. (2003). Religion and spirituality: Linkages to physical health. *American Psychologist*, **58**, 36–52.

Rainwater, L. (1990). *Poverty and equivalence as social constructions*: Luxembourg Income Study Working Paper 55.

Raleigh, M.J. et al. (1984). Social and environmental influences on blood serotonin concentrations in monkeys. *Archives of General Psychiatry*, **41**, 405–10.

Raleigh, M.J. et al. (1991). Serotonergic mechanisms promote dominance acquisition in adult male vervet monkeys. *Brain Research*, **559**, 181–90.

Ramsay, G. (1918). *Juvenal and Persius*. Harvard University Press, Cambridge, MA.

Rosenbaum, M. (2002). Ecstasy: America's new 'reefer madness'. *Journal of Psychoactive Drugs*, **34**, 137–42.

Rosenkrantz, M.A. et al. (2003). Affective style and *in vivo* immune response: Neurobehavioral mechanisms. *Proceedings of the National Academy of Sciences of the USA*, **100**, 11148–52.

Ryan, R. and Deci, E. (2001). On happiness and human potential. *Annual Review of Psychology*, **51**, 141–66.

Ryff, C.D. (1989). Happiness is everything, or is it? Explorations on the meaning of psychological well-being. *Journal of Personality and Social Psychology*, **57**, 1069–81.

Ryff, C.D. and Keyes, C.L.M. (1995). The structure of psychological well-being revisited. *Journal of Personality and Social Psychology*, **69**, 719–27.

Keyes, C.L.M., Shmotkin, D. and Ryff, C.D. (2002). Optimizing well-being: The empirical encounter of two traditions. *Journal of Personality and Social Psychology*, **82**, 1007–22.

Sandvik, E., Diener, E. and Seidlitz, L. (1993). Subjective well-being: The convergence and stability of self-report and non-self-report measures. *Journal of Personality*, **61**, 317–42.

Sapolsky, R.M. (1998). *Why zebras don't get ulcers: An updated guide to stress, stress-related diseases, and coping*. W.H. Freeman, New York.

Scherer, K.R., Summerfield, A.B. and Wallbott, H.G. (1983). Cross-national research on antecedents and components of emotion: A progress report. *Social Science Information*, **22**, 355–85.

Schopenhauer, A. (1851/1970). *Essays and aphorisms* (R.J. Hollingdale, Trans.) Penguin, London.

Schulz, R. and Dekker, S. (1985). Long-term adjustment to phsyical disability: The role of social support, perceived control and self-blame. *Journal of Personality and Social Psychology*, **48**, 1162–72.

Schultz, W., Dayan, P. and Montague, P.R. (1997). A neural substrate of prediction and reward. *Science*, **275**, 1593–9.

Schwarz, N. and Clore, G.L. (1983). Mood, misattribution, and judgements of well-being: Informative and directive functions of affective states. *Journal of Personality and Social Psychology*, **45**, 513–23.

Schwarz, N. and Scheuring, B. (1988). Judgements of relation-ship satisfaction: Inter- and intra-individual comparisons as a function of questionnaire structure. *European Journal of Social Psychology*, **18**, 485–96.

Schwarz, N. and Strack, N. (1999). Reports of subjective well-being: Judgmental processes and their methodological impli-cations. In Kahneman, Diener and Schwarz (1999), pp. 61–84.

Seeman, T.E., Dubin, L. and Seeman, M. (2003). Religiosity/spirituality and health: A critical review of the evidence for biological pathways. *American Psychologist*, **58**, 53–63.

Segal, Z.V., Williams, J.M.G. and Teasdale, J.D. (2001). *Mind-fulness-based cognitive therapy for depression: A new approach to preventing relapse*. The Guilford Press, New York.

Seligman, M.E.P. (2002). *Authentic happiness*. The Free Press, New York.

Shizgal, P. (1999). On the neural computation of utility: Implica-tions from studies of Brain Stimulation Reward. In Kahneman, Diener and Schwarz (1999), pp. 500–24.

Smith, A. (1759). *The theory of moral sentiments*. Edinburgh.

Smith, T.W. (1979). Happiness. *Social Psychology Quarterly*, **42**, 18–30.

Solnick, S.J. and Hemenway, D. (1998). Is more always better? A survey on positional concerns. *Journal of Economic Behavior and Organization*, **37**, 373–83.

Strack, F., Schwarz, N., Chassein, B., Kern, D. and Wagner, D. (1990). The salience of comparison standards and the acti-vation of social norms: Consequences for judgements of happiness and their communication. *British Journal of Social Psychology*, **29**, 303–14.

Strack, N., Schwarz, N. and Gschniedinger, E. (1985). Happiness and reminiscing: The role of time perspective, mood and mode of thinking. *Journal of Personality and Social Psychology,* **49**, 1460–9.

Svenson, O. (1981). Are we all less risky and more skilful than our fellow drivers? *Acta Psychologica,* **47**, 143–8.

Taylor, S.E. and Brown, J.D. (1988). Illusion and well-being: A social psychological perspective on mental health. *Psychological Bulletin,* **103**, 193–201.

Tiggemann, M. and Winefield, A.H. (1984). The effects of unemployment on the mood, self-esteem, locus of control and depressive affect of school leavers. *Journal of Occupational Psychology,* **57**, 33–42.

Tse, W.S. and Bond, A.J. (2002). Serotonergic intervention affects both social dominance and affiliative behaviour. *Psychopharmacology,* **161**, 324–30.

Turner, R.W., Ward, M.F. and Turner, D.J. (1979). Behavioral treatment for depression: An evaluation of therapeutic components. *Journal of Clinical Psychology,* **35**, 166–75.

Watson, P.J. and Andrews, P.W. (2002). Towards a revised evolutionary adaptationist analysis of depression: The social navigation hypothesis. *Journal of Affective Disorders,* **72**, 1–14.

Weinstein, N.D. (1980). Unrealistic optimism about future life events. *Journal of Personality and Social Psychology,* **39**, 806–20.

Weinstein, N.D. (1982). Community noise problems: Evidence against adaptation. *Journal of Environmental Psychology,* **2**, 87–97.

Wheeler, R.E., Davidson, R.J. and Tomarken, A.J. (1993). Frontal brain asymmetry and emotional reactivity: A biological substrate of affective style. *Psychophysiology,* **30**, 82–9.

Index